Killer Nurse

Life of Serial Killer
Genene Ann Jones

Jack Smith

ISBN: 978-1974094004

Printed in the United States

MAPLEWOOD
– PUBLISHING –

Contents

Genene Jones

Hospitals are where people go when they are sick, when they need medical help, or when they want to check on their health to make sure everything is going well. Nurses, doctors and other medical staff are seen as protectors who are able to help others get better. When children are taken to the hospital, parents are confident that they are in the best possible hands in order for them to get well. What they don't expect is for one of the very people who is supposed to help their child to instead hurt them, or even worse, kill them. It is absolutely terrifying when they realize they have put their baby directly into the hands of a serial killer who purposefully targets children.

Death is sometimes a possibility with certain conditions and illnesses, but it isn't usually expected – and even less so when a child dies in a way completely unrelated to the reason they are in the hospital in the first place. When there is confirmation that an intentional overdose of a specific medication was responsible, confusion and fear is quickly replaced by horror and anger.

Angels of Death and Angels of Mercy are terms given to doctors or nurses who kill their patients. Angels of Mercy kill patients who are going through pain and suffering. They believe that the person would be better off dead than living with the condition from which they are suffering. The most common victims of Angels of Mercy are the elderly and handicapped.

Angels of Death usually kill for very different reasons. Sometimes they lack empathy and kill merely from curiosity or because they can. Others have mental health issues or delusions about what they are doing. They may seek the adrenaline rush of a patient 'coding' (going into cardiopulmonary arrest) and needing resuscitation. They like being the hero when they successfully revive the patient. If the patient dies, they can then feed off of the sympathy from those who believe they tried their best to save the patient.

Genene Anne Jones (also known as Genene Anne Jones Turk) is labeled as an Angel of Death. Although officially convicted of only one murder and one charge of purposeful injury and harm to a child, it is believed that she killed somewhere between 45 and 60 children and infants. Genene had a habit of putting children in deathly peril so that she could be a hero and save their lives. Unfortunately, Genene killed many more than she saved, because her tactics involved over-medicating children either with drugs that would cause severe bleeding and cardiac arrest or with muscle relaxers that would shut down the child's organs, leading to suffocation or cardiac arrest.

Genene was an attention seeker. She suffered from Munchausen Syndrome, a psychological disorder that causes a person to pretend to be ill, or to make themselves ill or harm themselves, in order to receive unnecessary medical care and pity. When she wasn't seeking sympathy for her own created maladies, she was trying to save the day as a pediatric nurse, or to receive consolation when her patient died. She wailed in agony, poured on the dramatics as a distraught caretaker, and overall went from looking like an overly devoted nurse to someone with probable mental issues.

She was known for being boisterous, aggressive, manipulative, deceptive, and prone to hysterics. Injecting infants and children with heparin, digoxin, or succinylcholine to cause seizures or cardiac arrest, Genene would then proceed to revive them, yelling that they were coding or 'going' just shortly after they had seemed perfectly healthy. Sometimes the children would survive, only to be injected again during Genene's next shift. Other times, she would give them too much of the drug, or the damage would be too much for their small bodies, and the children would pass away.

It is often hard to understand why anyone would want to kill another person, much less someone who has taken the Hippocratic Oath to do no harm and works in a field with the sole purpose of helping and saving people. When the victims are children, the crimes become more appalling. When the killer is a mother, confusion grows even more. What makes a nurse who is a mother herself kill young, helpless children?

Genene was often seen crying at the bedside of a deceased child, or over the body as she carried it to the morgue. Although her tears seemed genuine to most, the truth is that Genene probably did not experience any sympathy or sadness over the deaths of these children. Psychopathic personalities have a hard time understanding human emotion. This makes them prone to causing both physical and emotional harm to other people in order to feel an emotional response and to receive an emotional response in return. In Genene's case, this personality trait was coupled with a level of imposed narcissism that had been built up over the years after a childhood of abandonment and self-esteem issues.

The first time a child was injected in order to cause an issue Genene could 'save' them from, it was both an act of curiosity about the outcome and a test to see how people would react to her if she saved the child. Once she received praise for her act of heroism, a new idea formed in her head. She was already known for constant complaints of physical illness. She would go to the hospital or tell co-workers she was suffering. Many assumed she was a hypochondriac and that constantly being around ill people caused her to believe that she was also ill. But Genene wasn't seeking medication or cures; she was seeking comfort and pity from those around her. Hypochondriacs really believe they are ill. Genene knew she wasn't and used false illnesses as a crutch for sympathy. She was a textbook example of a case of Munchausen Syndrome.

Not only was Genene able to get praise for saving a child, she was able to get sympathy when the child didn't make it. By playing both the hero and the heartbroken pediatric nurse, Genene was able to feed her narcissistic tendencies with the attention of those around her. Her inability to see the suffering she caused the families of the children she harmed and killed further testifies to her psychopathic personality and inability to feel true human emotion.

Why is Genene characterized as a psychopath and not a sociopath? Sociopaths rarely have the ability to express the human emotions that they don't feel or understand. Psychopaths are capable of mimicking or feigning such emotions in a passable fashion. Many times, though, these expressions are overly dramatic and thus end up seeming fake or like a sign of mental instability. Psychopaths are also known to be the more aggressive of the two personality types. Sociopaths are often seen as cold and unemotional, whereas psychopaths are often improperly or excessively emotional, since they are unable to express the correct and expected emotion naturally.

Some believe that Genene was a product of her experiences growing up. She was adopted into a wealthy family, but one with a reputation for shady business practices. She was one of four adopted children, two of whom died before Genene received her nursing license. She lost her adopted father in her teen years. Problems with children her age, conflicts with her adoptive sister and mother, a need for attention, and an inability to properly express emotion created a child with a lot of anger issues and a complete lack of empathy. Others believe her psychopathy could have been something inherent in her nature, since her biological parents, and their possible mental issues, are unknown.

Serial killers so often end up being the people no one expects. The polite family man, the handsome Good Samaritan, and in Genene's case, the pediatric nurse known for crying at the bedsides of children who passed away. Some of the people around Genene saw her for who she was, but some were completely taken in by her manipulations and the illusion she wove around her. Some saw her as a cruel habitual liar with no concern for human life. Others thought she was a caring, dedicated and competent nurse who was often targeted and misunderstood by those who didn't like her.

The truth was that Genene Jones was a serial killer.

Childhood

Genene Anne Jones was born on July 13, 1950, in San Antonio, Texas. For unknown reasons, Genene was put straight into social services, from where she was adopted by Dick and Gladys Jones. Genene was one of four children adopted by the Jones family, although two of her siblings wouldn't make it very far in life.

Dick and Gladys Jones were a wealthy couple. They lived a life of luxury in a mansion complete with a pool, horses and gardens. The means by which the Joneses had accumulated their wealth, however, were considered somewhat disreputable. The two owned and ran a nightclub by the name of The Kit Kat Bar. The place was known for treading close to the line when it came to legalities, and even crossing over completely with a side business of illegal gambling. The true nature of the business was more widely known than they probably realized, which resulted in a number of issues for their adopted children.

The club kept the family living large for quite some time. Dick and Gladys were known for traveling and enjoying the thrills money could buy. Both were licensed pilots. Sharing their wealth by adopting children was a good mark on their somewhat shady record. Unfortunately, the glitter and gold would not last.

After a decade or so, the club began to lose business and the Joneses began to lose money. Their property was auctioned off and a large portion was turned into a trailer park to try to regain some income. Although they did have tenants, the rentals still didn't do so well. Dick eventually got into the billboard business. He would drive around in his truck erecting billboards for companies looking to advertise around the San Antonio area. Genene told a reporter that one of her best memories, from when she was around 10 years old, was riding in the back of that truck while her father drove around town working.

Genene had two older siblings, Lisa and Wiley, and a brother two years younger than her, Travis. Genene was close to her younger brother. His learning disability seemed to garner him special attention and love from Genene, but she appeared to harbor strong resentment for her older siblings, especially Lisa. Genene saw Lisa as her competition. She believed that Lisa was favored by their adoptive parents and received special treatment. According to those who knew the family, however, Gladys and Dick were fond of all of their children equally and seemed to give no preference to one above the others.

Whereas Travis lagged behind most kids, Genene seemed to excel. On top her intelligence, she was also an adept seamstress, pianist, and baker, and she had various other talents. Despite the areas where Genene did well, she had a tendency to be less than friendly to the people around her, and she suffered in social settings.

In school, Genene was considered bossy and aggressive. (This wouldn't be the last time those words were used to describe her.) She sought attention, at times in ways that bordered on the obnoxious, but the slightest negative retort would put her in tears. Although she wanted to be the center of attention, she was unable to handle any form of criticism. She had a tendency to lie constantly and was rather manipulative. She told outsiders that she was bullied at school, but witnesses and fellow classmates were apt to finger Genene herself as the bully.

When Genene was 10 years old, her father, Dick Jones, was arrested for robbery. Originally it was reported that he had broken into someone's safe and stolen approximately $1,500. Other reports stated that he actually stole jewelry and not money, but there is no formal police record available that might reconcile the conflicting media accounts. Whatever the details, Dick was able to convince authorities that the robbery had been part of a joke between friends. He was released and cleared of the crime, but rumors of his illegal activities during his days as a club owner now had the confirmation of an arrest. Joke or not, his label as a criminal was solidified in the eyes of many people around the city.

As Genene got older, problems with her sister and her peers only got worse. Genene and Lisa were constantly fighting and butting heads. In fact, the animosity wouldn't lessen until Lisa was old enough to move out on her own. Genene was certain her parents favored Lisa over her, and that led to many arguments with her adoptive mother. She also claimed that classmates often picked on her because of her father's history as a gambler and his run-ins with the law. They also had a tendency to make fun of how she looked. It is true that Genene was a rather large girl and not particularly attractive, and her aggressive, bullying personality didn't help. Other children were either afraid of her or picked on her. This left very little room for friends and playmates.

Much of what Genene claimed to have gone through can't be confirmed. Many of her stories are not backed up by witnesses, and her habit of lying and manipulating makes it probable that many of them were exaggerated or completely fabricated. She would tell other people that she was picked on because of her weight and because of her father, but there weren't many who corroborated that. She would also make claims that she was abused; the biological daughter of a famous musician; hated by her adoptive family; and so on. She was a habitual liar. It seemed to come naturally for her, making up stories and standing strongly behind them until she changed them again later. What she did or did not go through can only be surmised from the people who were around her. From an early age, she showed signs of needing the limelight so much that she would do whatever it took to gain attention.

When Genene was 16 years old, she faced her first real tragedy. She loved and doted on her younger brother. He was one of the few people in Genene's life to whom she ever truly showed honest emotion. He looked up to her without any need for her to put on an act. In 1967, Travis was playing with a homemade pipe bomb he had been making. The bomb went off in his face and killed him. For the first time, but hardly for the last, Genene threw herself down in tears over someone's death. Whether the feelings were genuine or not was later brought into question when she displayed the same reaction to the deaths of the children she had killed. At that time, though, it was believed that Travis' death had a dark impact on Genene's life.

One year later, Dick Jones became severely ill. He was diagnosed with terminal cancer and refused any treatment for fear it would only prolong the condition. Shortly after Christmas, he passed away. Around that time, Gladys had taken up drinking. In the midst of this turmoil, Genene decided, despite her age and being in school, that she was going to get married. It is possible that, due to her inability to understand and show how she was feeling, marriage seemed to be the best way to deal with the recent losses. However, her mother refused to allow her to carry out her plan, causing more strain on their already tense relationship.

In 1968, Genene graduated high school and faked a pregnancy with her high school sweetheart, James 'Jimmy' Harvey Delany, Jr., in order to convince him to marry her. James acceded, and they were wed before she finally admitted the deception. Although her mother was against her marrying the high school dropout, she financed the wedding and the subsequent honeymoon. She also allowed the couple to live in one of the trailers on her property. James was a drinker and a partier, and Genene not-so-secretly liked to race cars, including her father's old El Camino. The couple fought constantly over each other's daily activities, and the marriage quickly began to fall apart.

James decided to enlist in the Navy after just over half a year living off of Gladys Jones, during which he had spent most of his time partying. Genene, already well known for her sexual promiscuity, promptly began sleeping with whomever she pleased once James left. She didn't hide the affairs, even those with married men, and was known to brag about them to anyone who would listen. She also began spreading rumors that she'd been sexually abused as a child.

As money became tighter, Gladys Jones had to sell off her land, including the area in which Genene lived. Genene moved to an apartment, but even then, Gladys continued paying for her home and lifestyle. She did, however, begin to urge Genene to seek a career and income for herself. After some time, Genene enrolled in beauty school. When James returned from the military, he worked as a mechanic while she worked as beautician in a hospital.

Genene eventually became pregnant and gave birth to her first child, a son, in 1972. Several months afterward, she filed for divorce. The separation didn't last long, and the couple was back together before the end of the year. In 1974, Genene once again filed for divorce. It was finalized in June. By 1976, Genene was pregnant again, with a girl. It's uncertain who the father was; Genene identified one man at the time, but later said that a tryst with her ex-husband James had caused the pregnancy. In any event, she would become a single mother with two children, and her job as a beautician wouldn't cut it anymore.

Later in 1976, Genene's older brother was diagnosed with advanced testicular cancer and quickly succumbed to the disease. Genene then began to obsess about having cancer. Every bruise, rash, or pain sent her to the hospital to be screened. Her fears soon had her worried about the chemicals she was always around in the salon. On the basis of a rash caused by the salon chemicals, and the history of cancer in the family, Genene convinced her mother to finance her way through nursing school so that she could have a safer and more lucrative career.

Since she had been working out of a hospital, she decided that a job in the medical field was the best bet for her. Genene had begun admiring the medial staff. She idolized doctors and realized that she could be close to them by being a nurse. The life of a medical worker would also allow her to delve deeper into her issues with Munchausen Syndrome and would give her a chance to be the center of attention when she saved the day. The job seemed like the perfect choice for someone with Genene's personality traits, and it was something that would easily allow her to feed her personality disorders.

LVN Genene Jones

Genene Jones decided on a Licensed Vocational Nursing certification. Although LVNs were not as high up in the food chain as Registered Nurses, the schooling was much shorter, and Genene was in desperate need of a job. LVNs also worked in closer proximity to doctors, and that was where Genene wanted to be. She dove into her classes and quickly showed a natural talent.

As she had in her high school years, Genene excelled academically in nursing school. And she had a similar problem with being rather immature, obnoxious, and constantly seeking attention. She was known for inappropriate jokes and remarks, goofing off, and being competitive. Using her hairdressing skills from her time as a beautician, though, she was able to win over a few female friends in her class.

She graduated with her class in May of 1977 and was officially a Licensed Vocational Nurse, ready to begin work at a hospital. Her grades had placed her near the top of her class and guaranteed her a decent position in the field. But Genene was also well into the third trimester of her second pregnancy and couldn't immediately start work. After her daughter was born in July, she left both her children with Gladys. In September, she began her career as a nurse in the ICU of the San Antonio Methodist Hospital.

San Antonio Methodist would be the first of several hospitals that would employ Genene before her arrest. Less than a year later, on April 26, 1978, they fired her. The reasons stated were her improper decision making in situations where she had no authority to do so and the mistreatment of a patient. She immediately found another job as a nurse at a smaller community hospital in May, but in October she had to resign to get a tubal ligation. Since she hadn't been there long enough to accumulate any sick days, and the surgery wasn't medically necessary, she would most likely have been fired for an unexcused absence if she hadn't quit.

Genene's third nursing job in a year's time was at Bexar County Hospital, now called the University Hospital of San Antonio. Possibly because of an ongoing shortage of nurses, Genene was assigned to the Pediatric Intensive Care Unit, or PICU, where the most severely ill children and infants were cared for. Nurses in a PICU are usually well experienced because of the delicacy of taking care of such small, young children and the stress of handling pediatric deaths. It is often considered the most difficult department for medical personnel to work in.

The first patient assigned to Genene Jones was an infant who was suffering from a terminal intestinal dysfunction. There was very little interaction between the baby and Genene during the short time she had him as a patient, but upon his death she went into hysterics. She moved a stool next to the deceased infant's containment unit and sat staring and crying over the child for most of the day. This caused concern among the RNs who worked in the PICU with Genene. The behavior showed an inability to handle what was, after all, a common occurrence in that particular department.

It didn't take long for Genene to make up for that first impression with her knowledge, eagerness to teach and learn, and her skill at putting intravenous lines into the tiny veins of the children. With children, the veins are small and the needles smaller, almost as thin as hair. Putting a line into a child is a delicate and precarious task. Incorrect insertion can lead to piercing the vein through and through, bruising the area, damaging the vein, hitting a nerve or a bone, and many other risks. Any IV insertion carries the same risks, but it is much harder to do so with children. Genene's skill was much appreciated and even called upon by other PICU nurses who had a harder time with the minuscule veins.

One nurse, Pat Belko, was very fond of Genene. Pat was the chief nurse of the unit and saw potential in the combination of Genene's skills and intellect with her nursing abilities and the devotion she seemed to have to the children. This came in handy when Genene came in to work one night intoxicated and was sent home after being discovered tampering with a child's IV. Pat Belko stood up for her, and Genene didn't even get a reprimand for the behavior. Other small infractions were also overlooked or downplayed due to Pat's backing. Pat believed that some of the other nurses were jealous of Genene or didn't like her personally and thus complained about her in order to make her look bad. Pat Belko had a hard time seeing the truth about Genene Jones.

Another champion for Genene was Dr. James Robotham. Dr. Robotham was the newly appointed director of the PICU, and he had made it his mission to weed out the nurses who weren't doing their jobs properly. Robotham had particular concerns about the improper utilization of medications. The death rate for the PICU was at an all-time high, and he was determined to find out why. He brought with him stricter and more stringent expectations of the nurses in the PICU. Prior to his appointment, there hadn't been a strong advocate for change, nor someone to push for the improvement of the department.

Despite Genene being the very cause for the initial inquiry into the abuse of medications, she immediately saw an opportunity, with the backing of Pat Belko, to steal the spotlight with her knowledge and techniques. At first, Dr. Robotham was quite pleased with her capabilities and aptitude. He overlooked the complaints of other nurses and focused on Genene's constant overtime and devotion to her patients. To him, she seemed like a competent and compassionate nurse, the ideal employee for the

PICU. Like Pat Belko, he believed that the other nurses were jealous of her skill. It wouldn't be until the hospital board became involved, after several dozen deaths, that Dr. Robotham would finally be able to see the truth about Genene.

True to her nature, though, Genene soon was letting the power go to her head. She began berating other nurses and bragging about her skills and her working relationship with the higher-ups on the floor. She began pushing the limits of her position and even overstepping her authority with the patients. Genene would refuse to treat a patient according to the doctor's orders, or she would apply her own idea of what treatment she thought the child should have. Her excuse was that she only did what was best with the child, although that was rarely actually the case.

Given her treatment of them and their growing suspicions of her involvement in patient deaths, the disgruntled nurses were eager to find proof of what Genene was doing and have her gone. Fellow employees began paying attention to the occurrences when Genene was on duty. They would report her for failing to comply with a doctor's orders or for tending to a patient she wasn't assigned to or when she was off duty. A deep rift began to appear among the nurses of the PICU.

Problems also arose with Genene's fabricated medical ailments. Within her first year at Bexar, she had over 30 visits to the hospital for miscellaneous medical conditions. On top of her own issues with faking medical problems, she also began creating false issues for her patients and seeking out doctors with her claims. She became well known for constantly calling in a doctor or intern for an opinion on something she had discovered. It rarely ended up being a legitimate issue. She consulted with the doctors much more frequently than normal, paging them up to five or six times a shift for these imagined problems.

Nurses are known for developing an ability to predict or expect when a patient will code. Just as experienced police officers tend to acquire an instinct for danger, medical workers seem to gain a similar ability to recognize when a patient is about to enter a downward spiral. Genene, despite her short time as a nurse, quickly became synonymous with predicting a code on patients in the PICU. However, at the same time, she also began to rack up quite a number of serious errors that would be put on her record.

Eight errors in the first nine months at Bexar was an incredibly high amount. The errors ranged from disobeying a doctor's orders to do what she thought was best for the child to giving extremely high overdoses of medication and everything in between. After an internal inquiry, Genene was twice required to attend a medical class on drug administration. She never went, and thus never received the proper training on drug dosage and administration.

Genene also began a bad habit of becoming obsessed with particular patients. In these situations, she would remain in the hospital to attend to the patient long after her shift was over. Even after being told to go home, Genene would refuse. The problem became big enough for formal complaints to be filed, but that did little to stop her from becoming so focused on specific children.

If one of the children died, Genene would make a huge production of the situation. Instead of allowing the child to be covered and taken to the morgue on a gurney, she would remove all the medical equipment from them, wash them, and swaddle them. She would then carry the child through the halls to the morgue herself, talking loudly in an almost mad ramble as if the child was her own.

As frustrating as her behavior was to some of the staff, others gave her commendations for picking up excess shifts and forgoing time off to help with the staffing shortage. Her odd behavior with the deceased patients was even seen as a sign of deep compassion by those who saw no harm in Genene.

As time went by, the staff became more divided over Genene Jones. The biggest tilting factor was the number of children she predicted were going to die, and the way her predictions came true with uncanny accuracy, to the letter. Her proclamations were often matter-of-fact, and they came out as unnerving to some of the other nurses. Genene was usually on call when the children did pass away, and she had made it a habit to make the sickest children, those most likely to die, her patients. She even went as far as changing patient assignments and taking over the cases she wanted without doctor approval.

Once, Genene jokingly told a co-worker that they were going to end up calling her 'Nurse Death'.

Suspicious Deaths

Eventually, several nurses began to get quite suspicious of Genene's ability to predict coding and dying children, as well as how she successfully resuscitated children on her watch far more often than normal. Her behavior with the deceased victims, the strange out-loud conversations she would have with herself and the wailing as she carried them to the morgue, was unnatural and alarming. The behavior was far from professional, and it was very concerning to the nurses who had begun to suspect Genene of having a hand in the fate of her patients.

Unfortunately for those nurses who weren't so fond of Genene, Pat Belko and Dr. Robotham were making it rather difficult to report her. Many who tried were accused of jealousy or trying to start intra-departmental drama. Because of the children she had saved, the time she put in at the hospital, and her skills as a nurse, some still saw Genene as a fantastic nurse and couldn't believe she would purposefully be causing harm to the children.

Many deaths and near-deaths popped up during Genene's time at the hospital. At first, they caused internal investigations within the PICU and the hospital. Later, those same instances would be important evidence in the case against Genene. At least nine deaths at Bexar in the year of 1981 were labeled as 'landmark' cases and used as definitive examples of how Genene killed, or nearly killed, many of her patients in the PICU.

On March 21, 1981, a baby named Christopher James Hogeda died from cardiac arrest. The child suffered from a congenital heart defect and was very ill when he became a patient under Genene's care. Only 15 months old, he had been admitted to the hospital for pneumonia and diarrhea that later became compounded with hepatitis and infections. Coming after almost half a year at Bexar, Christopher's sudden heart attack was considered suspicious. As with other deaths, Genene handled it histrionically. She was asked by the parents to sit with him until they arrived, and she did, but she also began her strange ritual of giving a monologue about her love and care for the child, crying excessively, and treating the body in an unprofessional manner. She removed the medical tubes and wires, washed the body, and continued her loud ramblings about the death of babies as she carried the deceased child around.

A housekeeper for the Bexar County Hospital, Rosemary Cantu, brought her daughter, Rosemary Vega, to the hospital for a procedure called 'debanding' for a congenital heart defect. The surgeon made notations in the pre-op paperwork about the child being alert and playful. After the successful procedure, Rosemary was moved to the pediatric intensive care unit. Her mother often worked in the PICU and thus was familiar with Genene Jones. Genene took over the care of the child, and shortly afterward Rosemary began experiencing difficulty breathing and had to be put on a respirator. She then began suffering from seizures. One doctor realized that someone had changed the ventilator's oxygen output to reduce the amount of oxygen being pushed through. By the next day, the child began to stabilize and seemed to be improving – until Genene's next shift.

Rosemary would end up having three different cardiac episodes. If she had survived, she would have been living with permanent brain damage. But on September 16th, she was pronounced dead. Journalist Peter Elkind interviewed Cantu and gave the following statement:

In an interview, Rosemary Cantu told me she had watched Jones inject something into her daughter's intravenous line shortly before her first arrest. "Everything was good," said Cantu. "I was sitting by her bed after the surgery. Then Genene Jones came on in the afternoon, and that's when it all happened. She walked in with the injection," recalls Cantu. "I saw her and asked her: 'What was she doing? What are you going to give her?' The [other] nurse had just left and took all Rosemary's vital signs. She said, 'I'm giving her something to help your baby rest.' After she walked out, not two minutes later, my daughter started turning purple. The monitors went off; people started running. She was doing good until Genene injected her. Then she started getting the code blue." After so many episodes, Rosemary's "neurologic status deteriorated to the point of being unresponsive to pain..." according to the doctor's narrative. Recalls Cantu: "I had to make the choice, me and my husband, to let her go, because there was nothing more they could do."

Jose Antonio Flores was a six-month-old boy brought into Bexar Hospital for fever, vomiting, dehydration, and diarrhea on October 10, 1981. While in Genene's care, the baby went into cardiac arrest. Baffled at the unexpected decline, the doctors ordered a brain scan to see what could have caused the sudden heart attack and profuse bleeding from all of his needle pricks and wounds. The equipment for the brain scans was down in the basement of the hospital. Genene took the baby there herself, and it was there that he suffered another cardiac arrest and died.

Nearly two-year-old Doralia Rios was brought into Bexar on the 22nd of February, 1981. She showed the typical stomach bug issues of dehydration, diarrhea, and fever. The child was put on a fluid IV of saline to re-hydrate her and antibiotics to fight the infection. Shortly after Genene administered the treatment, Doralia went into cardiac arrest and could not be resuscitated.

Dr. Robotham became increasingly preoccupied with his fear that improper medication was the cause of these deaths. His biggest focus was on the misuse of the anti-coagulant drug heparin. The majority of the deaths were from cardiac arrest, and the children all had severe bleeding issues when they died. Robotham went to his superiors and brought up the problem, instigating a closer look at the handling and distribution of medications.

A policy was put into place that two nurses had to sign out heparin, and meticulous notes and documentation were taken to ensure that the medication was not being abused, misused, or stolen. Any children who died of cardiac arrest and showed bleeding issues were to be tested for heparin levels immediately. The system seemed to work, and after a period of time Dr. Robotham reported that no problems had been found. Unfortunately, there was an issue stemming from one of his favorite nurses, and it had somehow passed under the radar.

The incident that finally gained the attention of the staff, and began focusing the spotlight on Genene, was that of the four-week-old infant Rolando Santos. His admission to the hospital on December 27, 1981, was due to respiratory issues. He was put on a ventilator and seemed fine until he went into cardiac arrest three days later. The child was taken for a brain scan and tests, but no cause for the sudden serious issue could be found. On January 1st of 1982, Rolando began to bleed from needle punctures and his blood pressure fell drastically. When the same thing occurred five days later, Dr. Ken Copeland was the attending physician for the PICU floor. He immediately had a test done to look for the presence of Heparin.

On January 10th, the infant again displayed the same symptoms. Dr. Copeland immediately had the blood test done again, and the results were the same. The child had a large amount of heparin in his system. Dr. Copeland was prepared and had a medication sent up to reverse the effects. On January 12th, he ordered the child to be moved out of the PICU despite his unstable condition, as he finally had definitive proof that someone was poisoning the children with heparin and that Rolando was being targeted. When he arrived later and found that his instructions hadn't been carried out, he angrily demanded that the child be removed from the unit immediately. Within four days, Rolando's health had completely turned around and he was able to go home.

The hospital board realized they would need to re-investigate the issue of heparin use in the PICU. Although several doctors and nurses were not quiet about their belief that Genene Jones was the sole culprit, there was no definitive proof. Fearing more deaths, lawsuits, and the media catching wind, they made the situation a priority.

As more attention was being given to the problem, a four-month-old named Patrick Zaula died from cardiac arrest after a successful surgery on his pulmonary artery. The death was unexpected enough that the nurses who had been present insisted on watching the autopsy, trying to find out what had gone wrong. Patrick's death brought a new group of people in on the problem of deaths in the PICU. Surgeons' success rates were falling due to the subsequent deaths of their patients after being transferred to the PICU for recovery. One department was killing off patients at such a rapid pace that the hospital as a whole was starting to get a stigma when it came to their care of young children.

Nurses became paranoid and were requiring other staff to double and triple check medications and treatments before they would give them to patients. Although there was a large contingent who were certain that Genene Jones was the heart of the matter, the investigation meant that everyone was doing what they could to be on the top of their game and to make sure that the suspected problem was the only problem in the PICU.

By this time, even Dr. Robotham was finally convinced that Genene was at fault. In her usual fashion, Genene made herself out to be the victim. She didn't hide the fact that she was a suspect, and she even confronted Dr. Robotham. When she asked, he admitted that he thought she was at fault as well.

Making references to a 'little black book' that she claimed detailed all the infant deaths and the doctors who had caused them, she tried aiming for blackmail. However, since the evidence clearly pointed to her involvement, no one was worried about the little book that may have or may have not existed. The threat seemed silly and histrionic.

When it didn't work, she took a different tack, reciting her dedication to her job and her commendations over the years. That, too, fell on deaf ears. Genene then resorted to claiming she was being targeted, used as an example or scapegoat for the rest of the staff in the PICU. She did gain some support from a few people who still believed that she was an innocent, hardworking nurse, but they were few and far between. Most of her co-workers had seen her lying and manipulation before and weren't fooled.

As the tide began to turn against Genene, nurses who had been watching her suspiciously worked together to prove her guilt. One nurse compiled a list of the deaths during the time Genene had been working at the hospital. Over half of them had occurred during Genene's shift, and she had been present for more than half of the deaths. The report listed 43 patient deaths in the PICU between January 1, 1981, and March 17, 1982. The patients were all assigned to one of 15 nurses, but 22 of those patients were Genene's. She was also present at the deaths of seven children who weren't her patients. That meant that Genene had been present at 29 of the 43 deaths that had occurred in less than a year. The numbers were much higher than a hospital of Bexar's size would normally see in that time period. With this information, the nurses were finally able to get the hospital's attention and have someone formally look into whether Genene was at fault in the many deaths in the Bexar Hospital PICU.

Finally, the hospital took notice and saw a serious problem. In their eyes, they had a nurse who was either purposefully or accidentally killing a large number of children with overdoses of medication. Their problem was that they had no way of telling whether she was doing so out of incompetence or if she was actually, intentionally, targeting the children. If they fired Genene for incompetence or brought charges against her and couldn't prove them, they could be sued for slander. There was also the risk that she could claim the incidents were accidents caused by her relative lack of experience. That would indicate that the hospital had someone under-qualified taking care of the sickest children they had, and that would expose them to charges of negligence.

After some deliberation, the board decided to make changes to the requirements to work in the pediatric intensive care unit. No one with less than an RN license could work in that department. Anyone currently there who didn't have one would be transferred to another part of the hospital. This was upsetting to the other LVNs who knew that Genene was the reason for the change. They all had to leave the PICU, and none of them was happy about it. Genene was, conveniently, unable to be placed.

As expected, Genene didn't leave without a fuss. Despite being labeled as capable of being rehired and given letters of recommendation, Genene still proceeded to cause problems about having to leave. She may have resorted to death threats, blackmail, and other harassing techniques to try and bully the staff. These tactics did her no good, and eventually she did resign.

The mishandling of the inquiries and investigations into the numerous deaths would still cause the hospital problems down the road. At first, they claimed to have lost over 9,000 pounds of documentation; finally they admitted to having destroyed the evidence for fear of being held liable for the deaths. If not for this reaction, Genene Jones could have been convicted of many more deaths than the one that would finally put her in prison.

Dr. Holland's Clinic

Dr. Kathleen Holland opened her own pediatric clinic in Kerrville, Texas in 1982. That spring, Dr. Holland called Bexar Hospital, now named San Antonio University Medical Center, to confirm Genene's previous employment status before hiring her. Genene's records had a notation that she was eligible for re-hire, which comforted Dr. Holland in her choice. Dr. Holland even rented a home to share with Genene and Genene's two children when the woman struggled to find a place for her family and pets in Kerrville. When other doctors or nurses approached her and warned her of Genene's past and the crimes she was suspected of, Dr. Holland didn't listen. She saw Genene as a hard worker who was good with children and a very capable nurse. When the clinic opened its doors in August, Genene was at her side.

Genene had met Dr. Holland back at Bexar when the doctor was doing her three-year residency. At that time, Dr. Holland was already planning on opening her own practice and was scoping out possible nurses to work there. Her biggest issue was the inability of many of the nurses to place intravenous lines in children. The other problem she faced was the expected wage for RNs. Because of her budget, she began scoping out LVNs to hire, and Genene seemed the perfect choice.

Dr. Holland was one of the physicians who often ran to answer Genene's pages and consultation requests when they were working the same shift. It didn't seem odd to her at the time that Genene was always accurate in predicting the decline or coding of a patient. She was also one of the few who admired the dedication and determination Genene seemed to have as a pediatric nurse – as well as her amazing skills with placing IVs in the tiny veins of children. Her discussions with Pat Belko reassured her even further. In her eyes, there was no proof that Genene had ever done anything wrong. There was nothing to confirm the suspicions that some of the other doctors and nurses were voicing.

One of Dr. Holland's first patients was one-year-old Chelsea McClellan. Chelsea had been born prematurely on June 16, 1981, to Petti and Reid McClellan. Due to her premature birth, Chelsea suffered from underdeveloped lungs with a condition called hyaline membrane disease, and she spent her first few weeks of life on a respirator in the NICU, or Neonatal Intensive Care Unit. Within 21 days, she was eating and doing well enough to go home.

Almost a year later, in May of 1982, Chelsea ended up back in the Santa Rosa hospital for breathing difficulties. Although she was officially diagnosed with pneumonia, all tests were negative and Chelsea was eventually sent back home with a warning from the doctors to keep a close eye on her. Chelsea's original symptoms had been vomiting and pausing in her breaths. Her parents were told to take her to the emergency room if the symptoms continued.

With Chelsea's specific medical history, Petti wanted a specialist treating her daughter. She knew that a doctor specifically trained to handle infants and small children would be much better than a general practitioner. Petti was therefore happy when Dr. Holland opened her pediatric practice. She made an appointment as soon as she was able, and Chelsea became Dr. Holland's second patient at her new practice on the morning of August 24, 1982.

There were discrepancies in the reports taken later. Petti McClellan told police she had spoken with Gwen Grantner, Dr. Holland's receptionist, to make the appointment for Chelsea in regard to minor cold symptoms. However, Gwen told Dr. Holland that the call had been because of Chelsea having respiratory distress and her lips turning blue. Petti would later be stunned at the misinformation passed to the doctor. She had even signed the initial paperwork listing her reason for the visit as a 'bad cold'.

Dr. Holland called Petti McClellan back to her office to discuss Chelsea. While they talked, the child began playing with things on the doctor's desk and fidgeting impatiently. Genene Jones was there and offered to take the child into another room so she wouldn't be a distraction. The women allowed Genene to take Chelsea and continued their discussion.

Within a few moments, Genene called Dr. Holland into the room where she had taken the young girl. Genene had an oxygen mask on Chelsea, who was lying on the examination table completely limp. Genene's only explanation was that they had been playing in the reception area when the girl had become unresponsive. Dr. Holland immediately began an IV in the child's scalp while Genene continued to administer the oxygen. At this point, Chelsea went into seizures.

Dr. Holland requested 80mg of the anticonvulsant drug Dilantin to be given to the girl. She then placed a call to the EMS to get the baby transferred to the hospital. Dr. Holland informed Petti that her daughter had gone into seizures and was going to be rushed by ambulance to Peterson Memorial. By the time the ambulance got her to the hospital, Chelsea was breathing on her own again.

Preliminary tests and scans gave no indication as to why the child had begun seizing and gone into respiratory failure. She stayed in intensive care for over a week before she was finally released to go home. Chelsea's parents were relieved. The couple began to tell people about how wonderful Dr. Holland and Genene were and how they had saved Chelsea's life. To them, the duo were heroes who had acted quickly and professionally to save their daughter.

On August 27, 1982, Brandy Benites was brought to Dr. Holland's office by her mother, Nelda Benites. For several days, the three-month-old baby had been passing dark and bloodied stool. Dr. Holland decided the child should be transferred to Sid Peterson Memorial Hospital to be put under observation. Before she left to make the call, Dr. Holland instructed Genene to put the baby on oxygen and to start an IV of fluids. Because of the diarrhea, the child was at risk for dehydration. In such cases, a standard IV of saline is started up to prevent dehydration and so the child is prepped in case of any emergency.

By the time Dr. Holland returned from her phone call, Brandy Benites' condition had severely worsened. The small child's skin was gray and her extremities were turning blue. Her breathing had become slow and labored. The standard transfer was suddenly turned into an emergency transfer. At Peterson Memorial, Dr. Holland wanted the baby moved to San Antonio to a pediatric intensive care unit. They intubated Brandy, set up the IV, hooked her up to the monitors, and put her in the ambulance. Genene and Brandy's mother rode in the back with an RN from Sid Peterson Memorial Hospital and an EMT. Dr. Holland followed behind in her car.

When the ambulance left Peterson Memorial, the child had begun to breathe on her own and seemed to be stabilizing. By the time they were halfway to San Antonio, though, she began to go into cardiac arrest. The EMT would later tell authorities that he was a bit thrown off by the way Genene acted. She began scrambling around and telling the child not to die, becoming very dramatic and unprofessional while they attempted to stabilize Brandy. Genene started a second intravenous line in the baby's foot. The EMT said they didn't have the equipment to do that in the ambulance; he therefore believed that Genene had brought it with her. They pulled to the side of the road and Dr. Holland joined them to resuscitate the baby. At San Antonio, doctors were unable to figure out the cause for the cardiac arrest and respiratory failure.

The following day, August 30, two patients ended up needing transfer from Dr. Holland's clinic. The first was four-month-old Chris Parker. His mother, a registered nurse, was worried about a condition he had called stridor, a noisy breathing disorder due to issues causing partial airway blockage. While they were in the waiting room, Genene came out to see the baby and stated that his feet were cyanotic (turning blue). She took the baby back to the examining room. Dr. Holland decided to transfer him via ambulance to the local emergency room to have his condition monitored. The child didn't show any distress and made it safely to Sid Peterson Memorial. He had a respiratory condition, but was stable. Nevertheless, witnesses said that Genene acted oddly. She stood over the baby, talking out loud about the possibility of him crashing at any time and acting as if he were on the brink of a code.

Chris Parker had been moved to the ICU when a seven-year-old boy named James 'Jimmy' Pearson was brought in. Jimmy was already in bad shape, and he had a rough medical history. He had been born with a fatal heart condition known as Tetralogy of Fallot. That morning his skin was ashen, his appendages were turning blue, and he was suffering from seizures. The boy had previously been treated in Santa Rosa. Dr. Holland was asked for her opinion, and she called in a request for a MediVac, a medical helicopter/ambulance, from the nearby Fort Sam Houston. The army helicopter arrived at the hospital to take the boy to Santa Rosa, and Dr. Holland requested that they transport Chris Parker as well. The medical technicians, Jimmy Pearson, Chris Parker, and Genene loaded onto the helicopter and left for the hospital in Santa Rosa.

31

According to what the medical technicians told authorities, the ride started out smoothly enough. The boys were stabilized and their condition unchanging. However, like many other witnesses to Genene's behavior in other ambulances, the technicians in the helicopter were uncomfortable with her demeanor. Although Jimmy Pearson seemed no different, Genene began acting panicky and claimed that he was deteriorating and seizing. The boy hadn't moved and the monitors showed no change. Despite the noise level in the cabin, with the rotary blades of the helicopter drowning out all but near-shouting, Genene put on her stethoscope and tried listening for Jimmy's heartbeat. At this point, the paramedics were genuinely confused. They knew she wouldn't be able to hear anything, and at any rate the boy was connected to the monitors. Genene pulled out a syringe and grabbed his IV line. The paramedics shouted at her to stop, not understanding why she would medicate him or what she would be giving him. As she continued to inject the contents into the IV, one of the paramedics radioed to the pilot. He requested that a note be made about Genene pushing unknown medication into Jimmy Pearson's IV and asked for the time to be recorded.

After the injection, the monitors displayed a rapid change in his vitals. He began going into respiratory distress before his breathing stopped completely. Then his heart stopped beating. The area in the cab of a medical helicopter is small in any case. Add an extra patient and a nurse riding along, and there is little to no room to do most procedures. Jimmy needed to be intubated, and to do that they had to make an emergency landing in a field. The paramedics inserted the tube and then pushed the stretcher back into the helicopter, which took off again immediately. The tube became dislodged, and the medical crew had to preform CPR and chest massages by hand while the helicopter diverted to the nearest emergency room. Jimmy Pearson was dropped off and the emergency crew took over while the medical helicopter continued on to Santa Rosa with

Chris Parker. Jimmy Pearson was then stabilized enough to finish the trip to Santa Rosa.

Genene told investigators a very different version of what occurred in the helicopter. Her explanation begs the question of her mental state. Did Genene lie in order to justify her actions, or did she seriously believe that the boy was in worse condition than he was? Genene claimed the child had turned "black" and that she gave him an injection to open his air passageways. She also told authorities that the paramedics in the helicopter had suggested she let Jimmy die. Her crass use of language, unprofessional mannerisms, and the fact that her story completely contradicted the two paramedics and the pilot was enough to make the investigators highly doubtful about her rendition of what had occurred. Although Jimmy survived the helicopter trip, he was never completely healthy again. He passed away on October 21, 1982. His parents sought legal assistance for a medical malpractice suit.

In less than a week, Dr. Holland's practice had seen more than double the number of pediatric cardiac arrests than the pediatrician had previously seen in her entire career. The numbers were quite worrisome, and Dr. Holland was left trying to figure out what was going on. Her new practice was already beginning to suffer. Fewer patients were coming in as word got out about how frequently children got sicker at her office. The parents of many of her patients believed she was a life-saver, but others were beginning to question what was occurring in the small doctor's office where so many children nearly died. Unfortunately, Dr. Holland's inexperience kept her from realizing the severity of the situation. Although she knew it wasn't normal to see that many pediatric patients crash, she did not know exactly how rare and abnormal it was.

The next incident occurred on September 3rd. 21-month-old Misty Reichenau was brought to Dr. Holland's clinic. The toddler had been experiencing a cold for a few days, and it had progressed to a fever. She also had sores in her mouth, and was now refusing to eat or drink. Dr. Holland began her examination. As she probed the child's neck and tried to get her to bend her head down, she noticed stiffness and immobility. Kay Reichenau was warned that her daughter's symptoms were common signs of spinal meningitis.

In order to get a confirmation, Dr. Holland would need to perform a spinal tap. The procedure would consist of having the child lie on her side while a needle was inserted between the vertebrae to extract spinal fluid. Pinkish colored or blood-tinged fluid was usually the first confirmation of the terrible condition. The procedure would be performed in a hospital setting in case something went wrong with the delicate maneuver, or the results were positive. Following standard procedure when sending a patient to a hospital, Dr. Holland ordered Genene to get an IV started and to push some fluids for dehydration.

Genene prepped the IV while Dr. Holland called for an ambulance transport. Before they started, Genene warned the Kay that children would often fight the insertion of the IV. Misty could make a scene that would be distressing for her, the mother, to witness. Kay Reichenau told her to go ahead anyway. The child did begin to fight Dr. Holland, but the doctor swiftly got the IV in place. Then Misty suddenly stopped moving. Her eyes glazed over and her breathing faltered. Genene told the mother that the child was holding her breath on purpose because she was scared. She made Kay leave the room.

Misty then began to seize, and Dr. Holland needed to get her intubated to control her breathing. Because the seizures caused her jaw to lock tight and they had a hard time getting the tube into place, Debbie Sultenfuss, the other nurse in the office, brought in a bottle of succinylcholine, also called Anetine. She told authorities that Dr.

Holland had requested the muscle relaxer, but Dr. Holland stated that she hadn't asked for it and told Debbie that she wouldn't use it because she didn't know the proper dose. The bottle was then placed nearby on the counter.

Misty was taken by ambulance to Sid Peterson Memorial and then flown to the medical center in San Antonio. When she arrived, she was stabilizing and the tube was removed. Tests and scans were done, but the doctors could not find a reason for the seizures and respiratory distress.

Sometime after the event with Misty, Genene told Dr. Holland that they were missing a bottle of Anetine from their inventory. Dr. Holland instructed her to look around the office, including the room where they had treated Misty, for the lost bottle. When the bottle wasn't found, Dr. Holland ordered a second bottle to replace the missing one. This information was crucial to the later investigations.

On September 11, Genene herself was a patient at Sid Peterson Memorial Hospital with complaints of an ulcer. One of her former LVN classmates was there and went to say hello. Mary Norris and Genene Jones talked for a bit. Genene told Mary that she worked at Dr. Holland's pediatric clinic in Kerrville and said that she planned to help start a PICU at Peterson Memorial. Mary had found the conversation a bit strange. She told Genene that the town's population and the hospital weren't really big enough to justify a PICU, which was why most children were flown to San Antonio or San Rosa. Mary also realized that Genene, who was only a Licensed Vocational Nurse, was not nearly qualified enough to run an intensive care unit at any hospital. The story sounded like one of the many that Genene liked to make up. But Genene stuck to it, telling Mary that there were enough sick kids in Kerrville to warrant such an addition if you looked hard enough for them. This statement ended up being a bit ominous, since the majority of children's deaths in the area would now involve Genene.

Chelsea McClellan

Chelsea McClellan was brought back to Dr. Holland's office on September 17, 1982, but it is not exactly certain why. According to the book *Female Serial Killers: How and Why Women Become Monsters*, Chelsea was there for routine immunizations while her brother Cameron had an appointment of his own. However, it isn't clear where the author got that information, and those who were present gave varying accounts of the reason for the visit. Petti McClellan claimed that Dr. Holland had asked her to bring her daughter in but didn't state why. Dr. Holland stated that "The call was not to set up an appointment to see Cameron. She told me that Chelsea had a cold that day, that she was having some funny little spells again – frequently. I didn't ask her just out of the blue to bring Chelsea in." Genene Jones said that Petti "had called in and told Gwen [that Chelsea] was having increased blue spells. She also stated she'd had two seizures that lasted three minutes each that day. She felt the blue spells were getting worse."

For whatever reason, Petti McClellan brought Cameron and Chelsea to the clinic that morning. Dr. Holland wanted to give Chelsea an immunization. Petti said the doctor told her she wanted to give her one shot, whereas Dr. Holland stated she told Petti she wanted to give her the MMR (measles, mumps, and rubella) and the Tetanus inoculations. In the examination room, Petti held her daughter while Genene brought over the prepared shots as Dr. Holland returned to her office. Genene injected the first shot into Chelsea's thigh, and the young girl immediately started shaking and having difficulty breathing.

In *The Death Shift*, Peter Elkind quotes Petti as saying, "I tried to tell her there was something wrong. She was just insistent about giving her another shot. I said, 'Stop, do something. She's having another seizure.' She said, 'I have to give her this other shot.' I said, 'Stop, do something now!'"

Genene told authorities that Chelsea was fine after the first shot and didn't have problems until after the second shot. Chelsea's mother, however, said that Chelsea had completely stopped breathing and begun to turn blue by the time Genene was pulling back from the second injection.

In court, Petti testified: "I looked at her and I could see she was trying to say 'Mama.' I thought, Oh God, she wants to say 'Mama.' Chelsea then went limp; just like a rag doll, just like Raggedy Ann – that's exactly what she looked like, just limp. She was still looking at me, but it didn't look like she could see me. Her eyes were all strange looking and they weren't like they were supposed to be."

Chelsea McClellan was taken by ambulance to Sid Peterson Memorial Hospital, where her breathing returned to normal and she began to stabilize. Dr. Holland was concerned that something serious was going on, but she couldn't figure out what it was. In order to find out, she decided to have the young girl taken to Santa Rosa Hospital for neurological tests and screenings.

One of the nurses in the hospital in San Antonio drove Petti McClellan and Genene back to Dr. Holland's clinic. While Petti talked to her son, she noticed Genene gathering various medical items into a bag. Originally, Genene had stated she needed to come back to the clinic for her and Kathy Holland's purses – although Dr. Holland was in her own vehicle and likely already had her purse with her. Instead, it seemed as if she was packing for another medical emergency, grabbing tubes, syringes, medication, and other supplies.

Back at Peterson Memorial, an ambulance came and Genene, a paramedic, and Chelsea McClellan got in the back. Dr. Holland, as usual, followed in her own car. She had issues with motion sickness and almost always followed behind the emergency vehicle while her nurse rode with the patient. Petti and Reid McClellan tailed the caravan to the hospital in San Antonio.

In the ambulance, Chelsea was stable, but still considered precarious. She was connected to an IV, a heart monitor, and a respirator. Genene and the paramedic took turns pumping air into Chelsea as they headed to the bigger hospital. Then, suddenly, Chelsea went into full cardiac arrest and flat-lined. The ambulance driver pulled over, and Dr. Holland rushed forward to assist in the resuscitation. Genene was told to administer resuscitative injections that consisted of sodium bicarbonate, epinephrine, and calcium chloride, while Dr. Holland continued with compressions in an attempt to get the child's heart started again. The ambulance was instructed to get to the nearest hospital, where Chelsea continued to code. More injections were administered, and CPR continued, but the child stayed flat-lined. Dr. Holland pronounced her dead at 1:20 PM.

While Dr. Holland went into the waiting room to tell Petti and Reid McClellan that their daughter had passed away, Genene began to clean up the body. She removed the tubes and monitor cords and then wrapped the little girl in a blanket. Out in the waiting room, Genene handed the body over to Petti McClellan. After a short period, Genene took Chelsea's body back and headed to the ambulance. Now a sort of funeral procession, the same three vehicles returned to Peterson Memorial, with Genene sitting in the back of the ambulance cradling and sobbing over the deceased girl. Cause of death was initially listed as cardiac arrest for unknown reasons; an official declaration of SIDS (sudden infant death syndrome) followed.

A few hours later, back in Dr. Holland's office, Jacob Evans was brought in well after his earlier appointment, which had been canceled due to Chelsea's transfer. The five-month-old boy was being seen for fits of crying that had been occurring for several weeks. His mother, Lydia, was greeted by Genene, as Dr. Holland had yet to return from Peterson Memorial. Genene took Jacob for blood tests that she said Dr. Holland had ordered. During the exam, Genene made a fuss about the baby's eyes. She kept asking about them and checking them. She told the mother she would be connecting an IV as well. When asked why, Genene stated it was a precaution in the event the child went into seizures.

Lydia Evans was unsure what to do, as her son had never had a seizure before and she had never seen any problem with his eyes. Genene then told her that she had seen movement indicative of seizure activity in the baby's eyes and wanted to prep him for transfer. She told Lydia to stay in the waiting room, saying that it was difficult for a parent to watch their child having blood taken.

Shortly after Genene took Jacob to the exam room, Lydia heard him crying and screaming several times before falling into a dead silence. Genene then came hurrying from the room, grabbed the phone, and made a call demanding that Dr. Holland be paged. Dr. Holland had told Genene to send Lydia and Jacob to her at the hospital and she would do the exam there. When she was told there was an emergency at her clinic, she hurried back, only to arrive just after Jacob had been put into the ambulance.

Dr. Holland asked Genene what had happened. She was told that Jacob had gone into seizures and the doctor and nurse from a neighboring office had helped with resuscitation after he had gone into respiratory distress. Genene also said the doctor had ordered 180 milligrams of the medication Dilantin, but she had only given Jacob 80 because the original amount was too much.

Dr. Holland stated later that Genene had rolled her eyes as she said this. It was never confirmed that the doctor had ordered any such thing, but it was typical of Genene to demean other medical professionals.

When they arrived at the hospital and Jacob was stabilized, Genene met with the family to give them the good news. Lydia Evans said that Genene was sweating and almost breathless. She said her eyes were wide and slightly wild, like she was excited and full of adrenaline. Jacob's parents saw Genene as a hero who had saved their son. Jacob would stay in the hospital another six days, but no cause was found for his seizures or respiratory distress.

Internal Investigation

While Jacob Evans was in Sid Peterson Memorial Hospital, several questions were beginning to pop up both in Kerrville and back in San Antonio. The number of infants and children suffering from seizures, cardiac arrest, and respiratory distress had reached biblical proportions. Some experienced medical staff had only heard of one or two such cases in their careers, and now there had been nearly five times that number in a very short period of time. Even more alarming was that LVN Genene Jones had been involved in every single incident. The children often recovered quickly – unless Genene accompanied them in the ambulance.

Dr. John Mangos was the new chairman of the pediatrics department at the University Medical Center back in San Antonio, the former Bexar Hospital. He was on a three-person committee investigating at least 94 deaths within a one-year time frame from 1981 to 1982, and they were in the process of finalizing their reports. The deaths had all occurred in the pediatric intensive care unit while Genene Jones was employed at Bexar Hospital. In 1983, the Bexar County district attorney seized these reports, which were later dubbed the 'Mangos Files', for the criminal investigation into Genene Jones.

The reports were narrowed down to cover the injury of three and deaths of ten children. They were all from unexplained bleeding, seizing, cardiac arrest, and respiratory failure. The reports' conclusion gave three possible explanations for the fact that Genene Jones had been present at all of the deaths: "This presence could be: 1) coincidental; 2) Because Nurse G. Jones volunteered in the care of very sick infants and children; 3) Due to negligence or wrongful doings by Nurse G. Jones resulting in the sudden deterioration and death of patients."

As San Antonio was wrapping up its investigation into the strange deaths and medical emergencies involving Genene Jones, Kerrville's Medical Management Board was beginning to ask about similar scenarios. Dr. Kathleen Holland's pediatric clinic had been open for less than a month, but there had been at least five emergency transports from the clinic to Sid Peterson Memorial Hospital in that time. It was an unprecedented number, and one that had the committee very concerned.

What was even more confusing for the medical workers at Sid Peterson Memorial Hospital was that, with the exception of the cardiac arrest that had occurred at the clinic, most of the children brought in hadn't been sick enough to have warranted emergency transportation. Once they were admitted to Peterson Memorial and stabilized, they had recovered quickly. All tests, labs and screenings they performed to try to find a reason came back inconclusive or negative for any possible cause they could think of.

On top of the alarming number of cardiac-arrest-related emergencies, the staff at Peterson Memorial were rather fed up with Dr. Holland and her nurse, Genene Jones. Complaints were made about the pair being demanding, condescending, and chaotic. As she had in the past, Genene Jones would brag about her knowledge of pediatrics, patronize other staff members, and boss around anyone she could. Staff had even caught her making notes in other patients' files. Despite their medical knowledge, when the two were coming in with a patient in an emergency scenario, the scene was unprofessional and unbelievable. What with their emotional outbursts, panicked reactions, yelling, urgent demands for tools and materials, throwing things, and all-out causing the most dramatic scene possible, they were nearly laughable as medical professionals.

The medical management team, though, was more concerned with the unprecedented number of near-fatal – and the one fatal – cardiac arrests that had occurred in the new pediatric clinic. They decided that they needed to look further into the situation. Dr. Holland was called and asked to come in to talk with the committee, which was headed by the chief administrator Tony Hall and consisted of the head nurse in the intensive care unit, Martha Carlson; radiologist Dr. Larry Adams; chief of staff Dr. Packard; and surgeon Dr. Schuster. A notice was also issued that any emergencies arising in Dr. Holland's office were to be carefully observed and monitored by the staff at Peterson Memorial so they could try to figure out what was going on.

Less than a day later, they had a chance to do just that. On September 23, Rolinda Ruff, a five-month-old baby, was taken to Dr. Holland's office by her mother, Clarabelle, for persistent diarrhea. Genene took the baby back into the exam room to check her vitals and hook her up an IV to use fluids to combat the dehydration from the diarrhea. Dr. Holland decided to have the child transferred to Sid Peterson Memorial Hospital for observation. As Dr. Holland went from the waiting room to her office and then the exam room, Clarabelle could see her daughter having an oxygen mask held over her face as she heard the garbled sounds of Rolinda trying to breathe. Rolinda Ruff hadn't even been fully checked into Dr. Holland's clinic. Her background information and medical history had yet to be taken, and now she was being loaded into an ambulance and rushed to Peterson Memorial.

The staff at Peterson Memorial got the call of a code blue coming from Dr. Holland's office yet again. When the patient arrived, accompanied by Genene and Dr. Holland, several doctors were already waiting to observe the situation. Dr. Frank Bradley, an anesthesiologist, was among those watching as the girl was rolled into the emergency room. Joining him were Dr. Packard, Dr. Adams, Dr. Johnston, and Dr. Merritt. The child was already stabilizing and her color was returning. She was trying to breathe on her own as Dr. Holland attempted to intubate her. Dr. Merritt told her there was no need for the procedure, but Dr. Holland proceeded anyway.

As the scene continued, Dr. Bradley watched the child carefully. She was trying to struggle away from the tube, her arms jerking as she tried to lift them. Dr. Bradley suddenly recognized where he had seen similar behavior. Anetine, also called succinylcholine, was a muscle relaxer usually used during surgical procedures. As the drug leaves the system, the patient's movements will be jerky as they attempt to regain control over the motions of their body. The child was showing signs of coming off of a dosage of Anetine, which made no sense to the anesthesiologist. (A side note on this claim: Although most books and articles on the case state that it was Dr. Bradley who noticed the effects of Anetine, court records attribute the observation to one Dr. Richard Mason.)

Dr. Bradley called over the other doctors and told them his suspicions. Dr. Packard went to find Tony Hall and tell him what they had observed. A committee meeting was scheduled that afternoon. When Dr. Holland came in for her appointment with Tony Hall, he told her that the meeting was about her nurse, Genene Jones, and how she was acting inappropriately and unprofessionally with his staff. His concern that Dr. Holland was somehow involved made him hesitant to mention their more serious suspicions just yet.

During the medical emergency with Rolinda Ruff, Genene had instructed Mary Parker, who had returned to Dr. Holland's office with her young son, Chris, to meet her and Dr. Holland at the emergency room where they were taking Rolinda Ruff. Chris Parker had been in the MediVac with Jimmy Pearson a few weeks before. Now he was suffering from an ear infection. After the incident with Rolinda, Genene brought Chris to a stretcher that had been prepped for an emergency. She had begun checking him over when a nurse told her she would need to take him elsewhere as the cot had been prepped for another patient. Genene commented about the possibility of the baby coding and hinted that the nurse would feel sorry if that occurred and she didn't have a place to take care of him. Within minutes, there was a code blue for Chris Parker. He had stopped breathing. The staff acted quickly and were able to stabilize him as Dr. Holland came in. Witnesses stated that Dr. Holland found a syringe that still had fluid in it near the baby. She asked where it had come from, but no one responded. Dr. Holland then evacuated the syringe onto the floor and told a nurse to dispose of the hypodermic needle.

Misty Reichenau was Dr. Duan Packard's patient. An older doctor with quite the history behind him, Packard was highly bothered by both the incident with his patient and the number of emergencies that were occurring in the small town of Kerrville. The problems continued to bother him throughout the day, and he discussed his concerns with a surgeon, Dr. Vinas. Like Dr. Holland, Dr. Vinas had done his residency at Bexar, now University Medical Center. He told Dr. Packard that he would make some phone calls and see if anyone there had any information that could help them figure out what was happening. One of his calls was to a resident in the PICU who recalled a spate of infant and young child deaths with similar profiles. The resident called him back to confirm that the nurse involved in all of the cases was Genene Jones.

On September 24th, the committee was informed about Genene Jones and the cases back in San Antonio. Dr. Holland was called back to the Medical Management Board for questioning. The doctor arrived well prepared. She had written down each of her emergency cases on individual index cards and relayed each patient's medical condition, symptoms, and the emergencies. Although the information sounded correct, and

47

each individual situation was plausible in isolation, the fact that all of the cases had occurred so close together in such a small place worried the board members. They then asked Dr. Holland about the Anetine. She admitted that she kept a vial in her stock, but said she hadn't used any since her residency at Bexar. When they inquired about her knowledge of the issues with Genene Jones back at University Medical Center, the former Bexar Hospital, Dr. Holland explained how policy had changed and all the LVNs had been relocated.

As the meeting wrapped up, Dr. Holland was paged about another patient going into cardiac arrest. Jimmy Pearson was coding in Genene's care, again.

The Medical Management Board decided it was time to involve a higher authority. They called the Texas Board of Vocational Nurses and told investigator Ferris Aldridge what was happening. He replied that it wasn't an issue for the Board; a child killer was a criminal issue that should be handled by law enforcement. Aldridge called the Texas Rangers. Investigator Joe Davis was the first law enforcement officer to be notified about the multitude of deaths that had been occurring over the past two-and-a-half years.

Several days later, Dr. Holland returned home from a short out-of-town trip. She discussed some of her meeting with the Medical Management Board with Genene, who complained of people making up rumors about her and causing trouble. Although Dr. Holland did not remember bringing up the succinylcholine, the nurse mentioned that she'd found the missing bottle from several weeks ago on her own. Dr. Holland had actually forgotten about it after having reordered the medication. She asked Genene where it had been and was told it was buried under items in the crash cart. Alarmingly enough, she also told Dr. Holland that the top had been popped. In other words, the plastic cap that covered the rubber stopper on the top had been removed. Dr. Holland asked if any had been used, and Genene said that there were no needle marks and both the original bottle and its replacement still contained the full 10 ccs of the drug.

The fact that Genene had brought up the very medication the board had been asking about began to gnaw at the doctor. Between the warnings about Genene, the odd occurrences at her former hospital, the repeated issues at Dr. Holland's office, and the questions at the meeting about her prized nurse and the drug that had been missing, Dr. Holland was beginning to wonder if she hadn't been duped all along.

The next day, Dr. Packard and Dr. Holland had a meeting in which Dr. Packard warned her that Genene was under investigation. If she wanted to avoid being pulled in, she would need to make sure her nurse wasn't doing anything wrong or making mistakes under her watch.

Back at her clinic, Dr. Holland went to her medicine cabinet while Genene was at lunch and looked at the two vials. The one with the top removed had two minuscule punctures in the top. When Genene returned, Dr. Holland immediately asked her about the holes and where the bottle had been. Genene reminded her of the emergency with Misty Reichenau and said that the bottle had been brought in at her request. The memories of Dr. Holland and her other nurse, Debbie Sultenfuss, contradicted each other on this point. Debbie said Dr. Holland had asked for it; the doctor said she had not. The Anetine wasn't used, though, and Dr. Holland asked what had been done with the bottle. Debbie recalled putting it on the counter in the room, behind the container of cotton balls, but she didn't know what had happened to it after that.

Dr. Holland was beginning to feel frantic and paranoid. The bottle of the very medication that was suspected of being used incorrectly on children who were going into a cardiac arrest had been misplaced and then found with puncture marks. Dr. Holland had to start asking herself if someone in her office, namely Genene Jones, was responsible. Multiple articles, books, and witness statements document the following exchange between Dr. Kathleen Holland and Genene Jones:

"That still doesn't explain the holes," Holland said. "How'd the holes get there? How am I going to explain the holes in the bottle?"

"I don't think we should explain them at all," Genene told her. "I think we should just throw it out. We thought the bottle was lost. We should say we never found it."

Dr. Kathleen Holland told authorities later that it was then when she finally began to realize how serious the investigation was and how probable it was that Genene was the culprit.

Genene Jones had lost her ally. As Dr. Holland realized the implications, she knew she had to do something. She called Dr. Joe Vinas and left a message, hoping he could help her figure out what to do.

While Dr. Holland was struggling with the realization that the stories and rumors about Genene Jones were looking more like fact than gossip, Genene had made a trip to the graveyard. Petti McClellan would later tell authorities that she had seen Genene at her daughter's grave. The nurse was rocking back and forth, moaning and wailing Chelsea's name. Her histrionics had been unnerving to the still-mourning mother. After her excursion, Genene returned to Dr. Holland's clinic. She approached the doctor and told her she had taken an overdose of Doxepin.

Knowing that Genene had been on prescription medication for depression, Dr. Holland had reason to believe this claim. Looking closely at Genene's face, Dr. Holland could see that her eyes were glassy and her eyelids were drooping as she struggled to keep them open. When Dr. Holland quickly searched Genene's purse, she found an empty prescription bottle for the anti-anxiety medication.

Hurrying to the neighboring doctor's office for help, she was promptly told "Number one, I am not an adult doctor, and number two, I wash my hands of this woman."

Dr. Holland called an ambulance and Genene was taken to Peterson Memorial, where they put her on oxygen and pumped her stomach. She had actually only taken four of the pills. Later she would say that she had contemplated taking more, killing herself, but had instead decided to go back and face Dr. Holland. (She eventually retracted this statement, apparently realizing that it made her look guilty; to this day she still maintains her innocence.)

Back at her office, Dr. Holland got a response from Dr. Vinas. After being told what she had found, Dr. Vinas made the trip to Dr. Holland's office. When he saw the bottle with the puncture marks, but still full, he called Dr. Bradley, the anesthesiologist who had first realized that Anetine was the drug being used on the children who were brought in to Peterson Memorial. Tony Hall also joined the doctors, and they proceeded to search the clinic for any information, paperwork, or whatever else could help shed light on the situation. To Dr. Holland's surprise, receipts and invoices for three, not two, bottles of Anetine were found. The third bottle was one she had never known about, and it was still missing. The first two bottles had been signed for by Genene, but the third had a blank signature line.

Genene Jones attempted to return to Dr. Holland's office after she was released from the hospital. Before she could, she was pulled in for questioning by the Texas Ranger, Joe Davis. Genene had no answers about the bottles but said she would take a polygraph if Dr. Holland would. When she arrived at the clinic, Dr. Holland told her that in light of her suicide attempt and the serious allegations, she was no longer working there.

Genene was enraged. Once again she brought up polygraphs, stating that she would take one and prove her innocence. Her emotions swung back and forth between angry and hysterical before she finally left. She called later to tell Dr. Holland to look in a drawer. Genene had left a suicide note stating the following:

There isn't anyway to explain to you why things are going to change. Sometimes, as wrong as it may seem, you have to except what life dishes out. When your older, and I know your tired of hearing that, but you will be able to understand why, why I have to go away. It doesn't mean I don't love you. Please believe that. No amount of money or worldly goods could ever buy my love. It is so deep & strong, it will last for all eternity. Please explain if you can to Heather & Michael how much I love them. It's such a strong love, I can't put it on paper. I know I'm asking alot, but I really feel your the only one who could do it. I'm not guilty of murder, & I hope you believe that. But Daddy's way is right. It takes all the pressure off you and the seven people, whose life I have altered. No one can hurt me with my Daddy. He'll straighten this whole thing out & then we'll go home & everything will be alright. No more problems for you, no more nightmares for me. Please make sure Michael and Heather are not separated. I know how my mother feels about Heather, but I also know how she feels about Michael. If Debbie or you can't take them together, please be sure whoever does are good people. People with lots of love. Please don't be angry. I'm going with Daddy because I miss him and I want to be with him. He'll take care of both of us. You'll be fine. Please believe that. I love you, Genene

Within the next few days, Dr. Holland's access and privileges at Sid Peterson Memorial Hospital were suspended pending the outcome of the investigation and Genene was called in for the polygraph. Dr. Holland stayed in a hotel, unable to return to the home she shared with Genene. Joe Davis took her in for her polygraph and then dropped her off. One of Dr. Holland's friends came by afterward to bring her belongings from the house. When Dr. Holland looked through them she found a letter and bottles of medication that Genene was trying to use to frame her for malpractice. The note stated that Genene had failed the polygraph and she was hoping Dr. Holland had failed as well. She promised that she wouldn't take all the blame for what had occurred and that she would make sure Dr. Holland would go down with her.

Trial

Both the investigation at Bexar Hospital, or San Antonio University Medical Center, and the Kerr County investigation into the cases at Dr. Holland's clinic and Sid Peterson Memorial Hospital were conducted mostly internally. By the time authorities were informed of the crimes taking place, both situations had been taken over, and looked into, by the respective committees. For the prosecutors, this meant that little leg work was necessary for the law enforcement investigation. For the children who suffered and the families of those that died, it meant that Genene Jones had been able to continue with her crimes long after she should have been stopped.

The difficult task for the prosecution was proving that Genene Jones intentionally injected the children with medications that caused their medical emergencies, and in some cases, deaths. In the mid-to-late 80s, forensics and toxicology had not advanced far enough to easily determine the drugs, or amounts thereof, present in the body of a deceased victim. This was especially difficult for those that had been embalmed. On top of trying to discover the exact drug and amount injected into the children, prosecutors also had to prove that the deed had been done with the intention of causing harm and was not merely a medical oversight or ignorant mistake.

There is little to no information available on how the case progressed from the Texas Ranger Joe Davis to the Kerr County District Attorney Ronald 'Ron' L. Sutton. Eventually, though, someone moved the case forward, and the D.A. began to dig into the mysterious illnesses and deaths of the children in a new pediatric clinic in Kerr County, a place so small that most physicians couldn't remember the last time a child had died due to a medical emergency. By October 4, 1982, Ron Sutton had enough information to go to the Kerr County Grand Jury. He began to present the case he was building against LVN Genene Jones for the death of Chelsea McClellan and the intentional injury of her and six other children.

As Sutton began working on the cases that had occurred at Dr. Kathleen Holland's clinic, Bexar County District Attorney Sam Millsap was wrapping up his investigation into at least 47 deaths of children in the 1981-1982 time period in the PICU of Bexar Hospital, now the San Antonio University Medical Center. Although Genene Jones was definitely the prime suspect, several other medical workers were also being interviewed and investigated about the incidents. When D.A. Millsap found out about the case being built against Genene Jones in Kerr County for the same crimes, he reached out to Ron Sutton.

Unfortunately for Sam Millsap, the evidence in Bexar County clearly showed that a lot of children had died, but it wasn't much use in proving that it had been at the hands of Genene Jones. Ron Sutton was having much better luck in Kerr County. The small clinic setting meant that only Dr. Kathleen Holland, Debbie Sultenfuss, and Genene Jones had had the access and the means to cause harm to the children. Of those three, it was Genene who had been with every child shortly before they went into cardiac arrest. Genene Jones was also the primary suspect in the cases back in Bexar County, and had been present for the majority of the suspicious deaths that had occurred there as well.

On top of the circumstantial evidence of know-how and opportunity, Genene Jones' mental history and the testimony of character witnesses backed up the belief that her behavioral patterns fit the crimes.

During the trial, Ron Sutton stated that her motive was to get a pediatric intensive care unit at Peterson Memorial and to possibly head the unit up herself. However, neither Tony Hall, nor any of the boards and committees at Peterson Memorial, had any plans to add a PICU to the hospital. Although it was a full-sized hospital, there were not enough children in Kerr County in need of such a facility to warrant building one. In the rare instance that a Kerrville child needed to be put in a PICU, they were flown to San Antonio. Even if it had been under consideration, Genene Jones would not have had any place in a Peterson Memorial PICU. San Antonio had removed LVNs from their PICU only because of Genene, but many hospitals preferred RNs and other more experienced and educated staff for the delicate and stressful PICU environment. However, despite its implausibility, witness statements made this the most viable and provable motive.

The Kerr County Grand Jury began hearings to review Ron Sutton's case against Genene Jones in October of 1982, while Bexar County began its hearings about the 47 suspicious deaths in February of 1983. Later that month, the information about the investigation into a possible 'baby killer' made its way to the media. On February 16, 1983, Texans learned about the possible deaths of nearly 60 children and infants and the intentional harming of dozens more through their local news outlets. Genene was starting to feel the pressure.

One of the witnesses for D.A. Ron Sutton was Cathy Ferguson. Cathy had lived with Genene when she was renting from Dr. Holland. After Genene had been fired from Dr. Holland's clinic, she had accepted an offer from the parents of Chris Hogeda – one of the children she was suspected of killing in San Antonio – to move to a trailer in San Angelo with them. Cathy Ferguson had gone with Genene.

Cathy had also spent some time at the clinic, and she testified that she had been in the exam room with Genene during some of her examinations of the young patients. On March 6, 1983, Cathy testified that on at least five of these occasions she had witnessed Genene extracting a clear fluid from a bottle kept in the top drawer in the room and injecting the child with the solution. Shortly after, they would get sick and go into cardiac arrest or stop breathing.

On March 13, 1983, Cathy Ferguson's one-week-old son was taken to the emergency room when he suddenly began having seizures. Though no charges were ever filed, it was believed that Genene may have injected the young boy as a way to punish Cathy for her testimony. However, it is also possible that Genene didn't know what Cathy had told the court. In that case, the action could have been a threat for her to stay silent.

In April of 1983, Ron Sutton caught a break with the evidence. Up until that point, technical limitations had made it impossible to determine whether Chelsea McClellan's true cause of death was an overdose of Anetine rather than SIDS. Because the baby had been embalmed before burial, investigators didn't think they would ever be able to prove beyond a reasonable doubt that the drug was what had caused her cardiac arrest and subsequent death.

But as it happened, Bo Holmstedt, a doctor in Stockholm, Sweden, had just finished developing a technique that was able to test for drugs like Anetine in an embalmed body. On May 7, 1983, Chelsea McClellan was exhumed. Tissue samples were sent to Stockholm, and within a short time Dr. Holmstedt's test confirmed that she had suffered an overdose of succinylcholine, Anetine, before going into cardiac arrest and dying. Ron Sutton had his definitive proof of the murder of at least one of the many, many victims.

On May 8th, Cathy Ferguson ate a dinner Genene had cooked and ended up going into seizures. If Genene was at fault, Cathy would be the last person she would harm for years to come. Genene Jones was indicted by the Kerr County Grand Jury on May 28, 1983, for the murder of Chelsea McClellan on September 17, 1982, as well as the intentional injury of Chelsea McClellan on August 24th, Brandy Benites on August 27th, Chris

Parker and James Pearson on August 30th, Misty Reichenau on September 3rd, Jacob Evans on September 17th, and Rolinda Ruff on September 23rd of 1982 while working at the clinic run by Dr. Kathleen Holland. Her bond was set for $225,000. Genene's response was to marry 19-year-old nurse's aide Garron Ray Turk and go on the run. She was found living with friends in Odessa and arrested. For a time, she went by Genene Turk; eventually she returned to her former name, but some sources still refer to her as Genene Turk rather than Genene Jones.

By November of 1983, Bexar County D.A. Sam Millsap had finally gathered enough evidence for the grand jury there to indict Genene Jones for the intentional injury of Rolando Santos on December 27, 1981. The devastating aspect of the Bexar County trials was that Genene Jones had apparently been responsible for between 9 and 60 deaths there, but the evidence to prove it was nowhere to be found. At first the hospital said they had lost the files on the suspicious deaths. Eventually, they admitted that the four-and-a-half tons of files, reports, and information they had gathered had been destroyed.

While there is no specific indication as to why the hospital did this, it is highly probable that they would have been facing a multitude of lawsuits (or a class action suit) if the information they had gathered had gone public. Their need to keep the scandal of a nurse killing children under wraps not only prolonged Genene's murders, but prevented the victims' families from getting justice later on.

At the beginning of 1984, on January 15th, Genene's trial for the murder and intentional injury of Chelsea McClellan, as well as the intentional injury of the six other children, began in Kerr County. Exactly one month later, after less than three hours of deliberation, the jury came back with a guilty verdict on all charges. Genene Jones was sentenced to 99 years in prison with the possibility of parole. In October of the same year, she was found guilty of the injury of Rolando Santos and sentenced to an additional 60 years with the possibility of parole. For many the sentences evoked mixed emotions. The nurse couldn't hurt any more children, but it had taken almost three years for her to be stopped. The number of children she had hurt and killed was a very painful truth that laid bare just how far a medical worker could go and how long they could get away with something so horrible.

Current Status

After the trials and verdicts, Dr. Kathleen Holland had to close down her clinic. She continued to practice out of her home, where Genene Jones used to live. Two of her patients, Brandi Benites and Chris Parker, were still seeing her as their primary care doctor. According to their parents, Dr. Holland was not part of, nor at fault for, what Genene Jones had been doing. They saw Dr. Holland as a victim in her own way, someone who cared about others so much that she wasn't able to see that they were using her.

The parents of Chelsea McClellan, Jacob Evans, and Misty Reichenau, though, had gotten lawyers and were suing both Dr. Kathleen Holland and Genene Jones for malpractice. Petti and Reid McClellan would spend a good portion of their lives fighting for justice for Chelsea.

Disappointment and aggravation with the missing files from the University Medical Center resulted in a probe into the hospital's investigation, the information it had gathered, and where the paperwork had gone. When it was discovered that the files had been permanently destroyed, the hospital claimed it had been part of a routine cleanup. The majority of the forms were pharmaceutical records, and the excuse had to do with prioritizing preservation of recent files over storage of older ones. It was then discovered that at least 25 tons of paperwork remained. This paperwork was seized by the Bexar County district attorney's office, and the hospital was eventually fined for obstruction of justice, impeding an investigation, and withholding information pertaining to a case.

Genene Jones came up for parole in 1994. Due in part to the diligence of Petti and Reid McClellan, fighting once more for their deceased daughter, parole was denied. Genene was up for parole again in 2009 and was again denied. Unfortunately for the

McClellans and the other parents and children involved, the Texas Mandatory Release Law then came into play. A loophole in the law allows violent criminals who committed their crimes between 1977 and 1987, and have served at least 1/3 of their time, to be released as a prison population control tactic. In combination with her 'model prisoner' behavior, that meant that Genene would be released in late 2017 or early 2018. A multitude of websites, Facebook pages, petitions, and outreach programs began pushing to have Genene kept in prison for the rest of her life.

On May 25, 2017, Genene Jones was brought up on charges of murder for the death of 11-month-old Joshua Sawyer due to an overdose of Dilantin. One month later, the grand jury had another case, that of the death of two-year-old Rosemary Vega in September of 1981, to add to the charges. Victims' advocates, the district attorney's offices of Bexar and Kerr counties, the media, and the people touched by the case were working diligently to help keep the baby killer in prison.

The Facebook page 'Victims of Genene Jones' is an amazing – and heartbreaking – display of people coming together to help those who were affected by the baby killing nurse. Survivors speak out about the health problems that have plagued them since their time as Genene Jones' patients. Families of those who were killed tell stories about the beautiful babies who never got to grow up. Investigators, journalists, and writers reach out to help look into the cases, spread awareness of the whole story, and keep Genene Jones behind bars. There are phone numbers and contact information for the prosecuting D.A.'s office and statements urging anyone with any information to come forward. Even renowned journalist Peter Elkind, the author of *The Death Shift: Nurse Genene Jones*, a 1989 book on the case, is on the page and continues to write articles and bring forth evidence about the killer.

Luis Castillo survived Genene Jones, but his life was forever changed. He constantly deals with a multitude of respiratory issues and other medical problems that put him back in the hospital time and time again. His wife, Amanda Castillo, stays home and helps take care of her husband, who now lives connected to oxygen 24 hours a day and will possibly require a double lung transplant. In an interview with the *Bandera County Courier*, Luis described the struggles he faces:

Meanwhile, here in Bandera County, Castillo lives with the aftermath of Jones' diabolical actions. He has struggled with numerous health problems all of his life, but "in 2007, I got really sick. I had a really bad asthma attack and my lungs started failing." Up until that time, Castillo had worked as an electrician and AC man. But it was hard to keep a job because of his numerous hospital stays. Today, he is on oxygen 24/7. He has been diagnosed with COPD, asthma, chronic bronchitis, pulmonary hypertension, congestive heart failure, cystic fibrosis and stage two lung cancer. His doctors have advised him that a double lung transplant could significantly prolong his life. Unfortunately, Castillo will have to go to Houston for the surgery. The day I spoke with him, he and his wife, Amanda, had been looking for an apartment in Houston. "The apartments are so expensive there. I live on Social Security Disability and we can't afford $1300 a month," he said. Castillo also has three children, girls ages 11, six and two. "They're Daddy's Girls," he said proudly.

With hope and determination, those who lost loved ones and those who survived move forward, doing everything they can to keep Genene Jones behind bars. Efforts have also been made to move against the people responsible for destroying invaluable evidence that could have forced her to take responsibility for more of her crimes. At present it seems unlikely that Genene Jones will be getting that early release date, but it is hard for the people hurt by her and the system to trust that justice will be served.

Motive and Excuses

The guilty party in the plethora of crimes against Texas children that occurred from 1981-1983 is Genene Anne Jones. She was a woman trained in the abilities needed to save lives, and she used that training, instead, to take them. There are still several questions, though. What was Genene Jones' motive? Was (and is) Genene Jones mentally ill? Does anyone else share responsibility for any of the events that occurred? Why did the hospital cover up valuable evidence that could have been use to prosecute Genene Jones?

The easiest of these questions to answer is the one regarding the actions of the University Medical Center, formerly known as Bexar Hospital. The basic facts have already been discussed, but the issue is still difficult to understand. The hospital was aware that something was occurring in their pediatric intensive care unit. Infant and young child deaths had escalated to an unprecedented number in a very short amount of time. The hospital did as most would do and performed an internal investigation.

Unfortunately, the doctor heading up the probe was Dr. Robotham, who had befriended Genene Jones. Dr. Robotham, and eventually the hospital, was aware that the center of the problem was the overuse and/or improper use of heparin. The medication was administered to prevent blood clotting, but it could result in severe bleeding and heart failure. The number of children dying from the symptoms of a heparin overdose was alarming. And yet, the initial investigation found no problems.

It wasn't until later, when Dr. Ken Copeland stepped in, that someone finally demanded the children be tested when they showed the first symptoms of a heparin overdose. Then the problem was laid out perfectly clear for everyone to see.

The hospital, at this point, was beginning to poke around a bit to find out who was the source of the problem. Dr. Robotham was originally supportive of Genene and doubtful of her involvement, but as various situations began to line up, he couldn't deny the coincidences. Dr. Copeland was already well aware of the possibility that she was involved. Pretty soon, the hospital couldn't hide the fact that they too knew that Genene Jones was the nurse killing the children.

But then they simply changed the rules to move all of the LVNs, including Genene, out of the PICU, believing that this solved the problem. They even went as far as writing Genene a letter of recommendation, placing a 'hirable' status in her file, and not progressing any further into their investigation of the many, many deaths.

Later, they would be held accountable for the fact that they had not only taken no action about Genene's crimes – had in fact supported her to help her continue working in the medical field – but had also destroyed evidence that could have been used against her.

Why? Fear of malpractice suits. Greed. Money. Reputation. The hospital administrators acted in order to protect and benefit themselves. Loss of clients, higher insurance rates, fines and civil damages, and the inevitable public backlash were not things they were willing to deal with. Instead, they buried their heads in the sand, which had the side effect of allowing Genene Jones to continue harming and killing children.

There are also many who believe that Dr. Kathleen Holland bears some responsibility for the injuries to her patients and the death of Chelsea McClellan. There is no evidence, nor much suspicion, that Dr. Holland was an accomplice, but there is a question as to whether she was completely ignorant of the actions of the nurse she hired. Dr. Holland was well aware of the incidents at Bexar Hospital. She was aware of the gossip and of the belief of a large portion of the staff that Genene Jones was behind the deaths there. Several doctors approached her and explicitly told her the danger they believed Genene posed. The other LVNs from Bexar's PICU had been reassigned, but not Genene. Why should Dr. Holland have made such a dangerous hire in the first place?

Dr. Holland's reasoning was budget. She couldn't afford to pay a nurse with higher qualifications or more experience. She was also reported as saying how impressed she was with Genene's skill at inserting IV lines into children. However, even if one accepts that reasoning, there is the further issue of why Genene was given such a high level of access and permissions for the care of the children when she had such a questionable history. And even excusing both the hiring decision and the freedom she gave the nurse, there is still the fact that Dr. Holland had trained in pediatrics. Her office produced more pediatric cardiac arrests in a few weeks than the whole county had in years, but at no point did she seem to find that suspicious. Nor did she seem suspicious of Genene injecting each patient with something, even if it was just hooking them up to IV fluids, prior to each code.

The questions raised by these facts may never be answered. There isn't much information on the lawsuits against Dr. Holland by some of the victims' families. Neither has there been any explanation from Dr. Holland as to why she didn't realize that the events that occurred in her office were problematic, much less why she failed to identify the source of those problems.

In any case, the primary guilty party, the actual murderer, was Genene Jones. Although she was able to get away with much, much more than she should have, she was eventually caught, tried, found guilty, and sentenced to a life behind bars. Her early release is a possibility, but one that is becoming less likely as more evidence is uncovered and more information about other deaths is tied to her.

The question is, though, why? Her need for attention, her desire to be a hero, and her hope of getting a PICU opened at Peterson Memorial have already been discussed. However, many clues in her behavior make these seem more like rationalizations than a full justification for why a healthcare worker and mother would kill several dozen children (even if she did attempt to resuscitate some of them).

The probable answer to the 'why' of Genene Anne Jones' crimes is two related conditions: Munchausen Syndrome and Munchausen Syndrome by Proxy. The conditions are still somewhat disputed in psychological circles, as they are at the same time broad terms used to discuss a cluster of mental issues and very specific terms that provide a medical explanation for a person's actions. According to Dr. Marc Feldman's website on Munchausen: "People with factitious disorder and Munchausen syndrome feign, exaggerate, or actually self-induce illnesses. Their aim? To assume the status of 'patient,' and thereby to win attention, nurturance, and lenience from professionals or nonprofessionals that they feel unable to obtain in any other way."

From an early age, Genene Jones showed a penchant for doing anything she could for attention. Despite her love and adoration for her disabled younger brother Travis, the attention he received from her could have been a gateway that showed her how illness can provoke a specific response to people. This was then bolstered by watching both her father and older brother go through cancer, the doting medical staff, and then the sympathy and support people gave her and her family when they were mourning the loss. It was while her father and older brother were dying that Genene began to become interested in the medical field. With her older brother, she became fascinated with the respect and authority that the doctors had. This was reinforced when she started working as a beautician in a hospital, where she was also able to see how nurses fit into the same pattern and rhythm. They didn't get the same attention, but the patients did, in their own fashion. Once she became a nurse, it was easy to see how family gathered around a patient, how doctors and nurses took care of them.

Genene had a three-pronged approach for getting this attention, respect, and show of emotions. The first was to be a victim, a patient, to claim suffering on a mental and physical level. She claimed disease, illness, and medical problems requiring hospitals and doctors. She also used claims of abuse, sexual and physical, to explain her emotional issues and to gain more support. The second angle was using her status as a medical professional. This got her both attention and respect, and when a patient died, she was also a victim, someone needing comfort. The third path was using her job to both claim fake illnesses herself and actually cause illnesses in her patients to get attention. Her responses to these emergencies got her respect and put people in awe of her abilities. When her patient passed away, and she played the role of heartbroken and dedicated preserver of life, she received sympathy, sometimes from the very family members of the children she hurt or killed.

Munchausen Syndrome by Proxy usually occurs when a child's parent or caretaker makes a child ill, or pretends that the child is ill or sicker than they actually are. Genene Jones was an odd case in that she did this with her patients, with other people's children. With her abilities at manipulation, she was able to gain the sympathy and understanding usually reserved for a child's parents.

Genene Jones is a habitual liar, master manipulator, and a textbook psychopath. Since psychopathy is not a psychological diagnosis, the medically accepted term for her mental problem is Antisocial Personality Disorder. People with this disorder have difficulty properly socializing and interacting with other people. This leads them to mirror emotions they see in others or display emotions they guess may be appropriate. In some cases, such as Genene's, these emotions are overdone or dramatized. Depression and antisocial behaviors are conducive to Munchausen and Munchausen by Proxy. In Genene Jones, the combination of these issues and inabilities formed the perfect storm to create a mentality that was able to justify the deaths of children in order to attract attention and sympathy. Early diagnosis and treatment of people with such issues must be done to prevent them from evolving into a danger to society. Genene not only wasn't treated; she was enabled to continue using the devastating tactics she had found to gain the attention that she wanted in her life.

Appendix 1
Known Victims

Identifying the victims of Genene Jones is a difficult task. Medical records are confidential, children's records are confidential, and records being utilized in a trial or investigation are often confidential as well. This is why Genene's total number of victims could be anywhere from 11 to 60. The following list is based on information obtained through various articles, books, petitions, and social media sites. Some of the information may suffer from inaccuracies as there is no official documentation to back it up and confirm the dates, names, and circumstances.

Benites, Brandy – August 27, 1982, 1 month old, survived overdose of succinylcholine. Current status unknown.

Castillo, Luis – March 1981, survived overdose. Currently physically handicapped with a multitude of health problems. Recently went public about his struggles.

Estrada, Jose – October 10, 1981, died from possible heparin overdose.

Evans, Jacob – September 17, 1982, 5 months old, survived overdose of succinylcholine.

Flores, Jose Antonio – October 10, 1981, 6 months old, died from cardiac arrest caused by an overdose of heparin.

Garza, Albert – 1981, died from cardiac arrest.

Hogeda, Christopher James – May 21, 1981, 15 months old, died from cardiac arrest.

McClellan, Chelsea – September 17, 1982, 15 months old, died from succinylcholine overdose. Only murder that Genene Jones was originally charged for. Her mother and father have been the strongest activists and voices against Genene Jones. Her mother now has several Facebook pages and petitions, and is constantly fighting for justice for the victims.

Parker, Chris – September 23, 1982, 4 months old, survived an overdose of succinylcholine.

Pearson, James 'Jimmy' – August 30, 1982, 7 years old, initially survived overdose of succinylcholine but died in October of 1982 after being unable to fully recover from the damage caused.

Planas, Tammy Rene – 1981, died from cardiac arrest.

Reichenau, Misty – September 3, 1982, 21 months old, survived an overdose of succinylcholine. Now married and now going by her married name. She and her mother recently went to the media to speak out against the possible release of Genene Jones.

Rios, Doralia – December 22, 1981, 25 months old, died from cardiac arrest.

Rodriguez, Feliciano – 1981, 5 months old, died from cardiac arrest. His mother Marina Rodriguez has come forward to join Petti McClellan and survivor Rolando Santos in fighting to keep Jones in prison.

Ruff, Rolinda – September 23, 1982, 5 months old, survived an overdose of succinylcholine.

Santos, Rolando – December 27, 1981, 4 weeks old, survived a multitude of injections and overdose attempts with the drug heparin. Genene's second sentence for 60 years was for the intentional injuring of Rolando Santos. Rolando is now an advocate for the survivors and victims of Genene Jones.

Sawyer, Joshua – 1981, 11 months old, died from an overdose of Dilantin. One of two murders for which Genene Jones has recently been indicted, potentially preventing her early release from prison.

Vega, Rosemary – September 16, 1981, 2 years old, died from cardiac arrest. Second of the two murders that Genene Jones has been indicted in recently, potentially preventing her early release from prison.

Villela, Jeffrey – October, 1981, several weeks old, survived cardiac arrest. He has currently begun speaking on social media about the case.

Zaula, Patrick – January 17, 1982, 4 months old, died due to an overdose on heparin.

Appendix 2
Timeline

1950 – Genene Anne Jones is born on July 13 and put up for adoption. Nightclub owners Dick and Gladys Jones adopt Genene, who will become one of four adopted children in the family.

1960 – Dick Jones is arrested for burglary, but the charges are later dropped. The Joneses' financial difficulties lead them to start a billboard business. Genene starts acting out by faking illnesses and causing problems in school.

1968 – 14-year-old Travis (Genene's closest sibling in age and relationship) is accidentally killed while building a pipe bomb. Genene makes her first dramatic scene in response to a death. Later that year, Dick Jones is diagnosed with terminal cancer but refuses treatment and dies shortly after Christmas. Genene reacts by deciding to get married young, but her mother refuses to allow her to and begins drinking heavily. That fall, Genene marries James Harvey DeLany Jr. after faking a pregnancy.

1969 – James DeLany enlists in the Navy. Genene becomes unfaithful and promiscuous, starts making false sexual abuse allegations about her childhood, and enrolls in beauty school.

1972 – In January Genene gives birth to James DeLany's son. In June, Genene files for divorce, but in September she and James reconcile and get back together.

1974 – In February, Genene once again files for divorce, while James is in the hospital following a boating accident. Genene claims domestic abuse as the reason for separation. In June, the divorce finalized.

1976 – Genene is pregnant with her second child. Her older brother passes away from testicular cancer. She decides to pursue a Licensed Vocational Nursing certification.

1977 – In May, Genene completes her schooling. She gives birth to her daughter in July and begins working at San Antonio's Methodist Hospital a few months later.

1978 – Genene is fired from Methodist Hospital in April for failing to follow orders and improper conduct with a patient. In May she begins working at a private hospital, from which she resigns in October when she has elective surgery to have her tubes tied. In November she begins working at Bexar Hospital in the Pediatric Intensive Care Unit. Within a few days she loses her first patient, to intestinal cancer, and doesn't seem to take the death well. In her first year at Bexar, Genene makes eight medical errors involving medication and treatment choices. However, she is defended by supervising nurse Pat Belko, and she gains confidence in her position. Dr. James Robotham becomes the director of the PICU and begins monitoring the use of medications on its young patients. Genene is seen in the hospital as a patient over 30 times for faked illnesses and conditions.

1981 – In May, Christopher James Hogeda dies from cardiac arrest. The death of Jose Antonio Flores from cardiac arrest caused by a heparin overdose occurs in October. On December 22nd, Doralia Rios from dies from cardiac arrest. Rolando Santos is admitted to hospital for pneumonia on December 27th. On December 30th he has unexplained seizures.

1982 – On New Year's Day, Rolando begins suffering from severe bleeding from a possible heparin overdose. On the 6th of January, he has more bleeding, which is confirmed as a heparin overdose. On the 10th, Rolando once again suffers more bleeding from another heparin overdose. Dr. Copeland has Rolando removed from the PICU on January 12th. On January

16th, Rolando goes home healthy. On January 17th, Patrick Zaula dies of a heparin overdose and Dr. Robotham and the board begin internal inquiries resulting in Genene Jones' resignation. In the spring, Dr. Kathleen Holland, who is planning to start her own clinic, hires Genene Jones to work for her once the doors are opened. On August 23rd, Genene starts working at Dr. Holland's clinic. In mid-August, Chelsea McClellan comes in for a check-up and goes into cardiac arrest but survives. Brandy Benites suffers from unexplained respiratory distress on August 27th. Jimmy Pearson goes into cardiac arrest on August 30th, and Misty Reichenau goes into cardiac arrest on September 3rd. Genene goes to hospital for an ulcer on September 11th. On September 17th, Chelsea McClellan comes in for regular immunizations and dies from cardiac arrest. Later that same day, Jacob Evans goes into respiratory distress. The Medical Management Board begins looking into Dr. Holland's practice on September 22nd. Rolinda Ruff and Chris Parker go into cardiac arrest on September 23rd. The next day, the Medical Management Board meets with Dr. Holland. On September 25th, Dr. Holland finds drug vials that have been tampered with. She fires Genene on September 28th. The first court hearing on the eight children who were injured and the death of Chelsea McClellan occurs on October 12th in Kerr County.

1983 – In February, the Bexar County Grand Jury begins hearings on the 47 suspicious deaths at Bexar Hospital that occurred during Genene's shifts. Genene marries a 19-year-old male nurse and goes on the run for a short time before she is indicted for murder and held on $225,000 bond in Kerr County. In November, the Bexar County Grand Jury indicts Genene for injuring Rolando Santos.

1984 – The trial for the murder of Chelsea McClellan and the injury of several other children begins in January. On February 15th, there is a three-hour deliberation before the jury returns with a guilty verdict and sentences Genene Jones to 99 years in prison with the possibility of parole for the death of Chelsea McClellan. In October, at the trial for the injury of Rolando Santos, the jury comes to a guilty verdict and sentences her to 60 years, concurrent with the previous 99 and with the possibility of parole.

1994 – Jones is denied parole based on pleas by the family of Chelsea McClellan.

2009 – Jones is once again denied parole.

2017 – Genene Jones is scheduled for early release in late 2017 or early 2018 due to the Texas Mandatory Release Law. On May 25th, Genene is indicted for the death of 11-month-old Joshua Sawyer. On June 21st, Genene is indicted for the death of two-year-old Rosemary Vega.

Appendix 3
Further Reading and Information

Books:

Deadly Medicine (1988) by Kelly Moore and Dan Reed

Female Serial Killers: How and Why Women Become Monsters (2007) by Peter Vronsky

The Death Shift (1990) by Peter Elkind

The Killer Nurse: The True Story of Genene Jones (2016) by Kori Mayer

We Are Here to Kill You (2017) by Tami Barrera

Documentaries

American Monster Discovery Channel Documentary

Deadly Women "Dark Secrets" Season 2 Episode 4 by Investigation Discovery

Forensic Files "Nursery Crimes" Season 2

Lethal Injection Discovery Channel Documentary

Raising America Investigates: Genene Jones

Movies Based on or influenced by the case

Deadly Medicine (1991) Genene Jones portrayed by Susan Ruttan

Stephen King's Misery (1990)

Appendix 4
Medical Terminology

<u>Anetine</u> – See Succinylcholine.

<u>Calcium Chloride</u> – Used to quickly increase calcium levels in blood plasma, often used in resuscitation when epinephrine is ineffective.

<u>Cardiac Arrest</u> – When the heart suddenly and completely stops beating.

<u>Congenital</u> – A medical condition or problem one is born with.

<u>Dilantin</u> – Anti-epileptic or anticonvulsant drug used to control seizures.

<u>Epinephrine</u> – Contracts the blood vessels and expands airways in the lungs.

<u>Hyaline Membrane Disease</u> – Also known as Respiratory Distress Syndrome (RDS). Occurs in newborns, usually premature babies, when their lungs have not formed enough to allow for proper respiration.

<u>Sodium Bicarbonate</u> – Used to balance metabolic acidosis, usually in the case of acid indigestion; however, concentrated injections can utilize lactic acid to help the heart deal with tissue acidity following a cardiac arrest.

<u>Stridor</u> – When breathing is accompanied by a high pitch and/or loud sound due to airways that are partially obstructed.

<u>Succinylcholine</u> – A very powerful muscle relaxant.

<u>Tetralogy of Fallot</u> – Congenital heart defect that causes issues with blood flow in the heart and lungs resulting in oxygen-poor blood. Occurs in 5 of every 10,000 infants and usually necessitates open-heart surgery.

References

Blanco, Juan Ignacio. "Genene Anne JONES." Genene Jones | Murderpedia, the   encyclopedia of murderers. Accessed June 20, 2017.   http://murderpedia.org/female.J/j/jones-genene.htm.

Edwards, Carolyn B. "Local survived 80s serial killer attack." *Bandera Courier* Article.   June 22, 2017. Accessed June 23, 2017.
http://www.bccourier.com/Archives/News_detail.php?cont entId=14832.

Elkind, Peter. "The "Angel-of-Death" Nurse Charged with Death of Second Baby." *Texas Monthly.* June 21, 2017. Accessed June 25, 2017.   http://www.texasmonthly.com/the-daily-post/angel-death-nurse-charged-death- second-baby/.

Elkind, Peter. "The Death Shift." *Texas Monthly.* August 1983. Accessed   June   20,   2017.
http://www.texasmonthly.com/articles/the-death-shift-2/.

Feldman, Dr. Marc. "Munchausen Syndrome." Munchausens. Accessed June 21, 2017. http://munchausen.com/.

Jones VS Texas (1986), No. 716 S.W.2d 142 (Tex. App. 1986) slip op. at No. 3-84-200- CR. (Court of Appeals of Texas, Austin.).

"National Institutes of Health." National Institutes of Health. Accessed June 21, 2017. https://www.nih.gov/.

"Personality Spotlight; NEWLN: Nurse Genene Jones: Convicted murderer." UPI.   February 15, 1984. Accessed June   20,   2017.   http://www.upi.com/Archives/1984/02/15/Personality-SpotlightNEWLNNurse-   Genene-Convicted-murderer/6881445669200/.

"Prescription Drug Information, Interactions & Side Effects." Drugs.com. Accessed June   21,   2017. https://www.drugs.com/.

Vronsky, Peter. *Female Serial Killers: How and Why Women Become Monsters*. New York: Penguin, 2007.

XL, RealFrenz. "True Crime XL." Genene Jones – Baby Killer. August 03, 2012.   Accessed   June   20,   2017. http://truecrimecases.blogspot.com/2012/08/genene- jones-baby-killer.html.

Also by Jack Smith

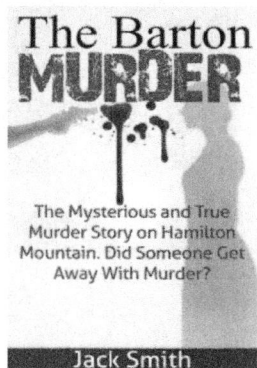

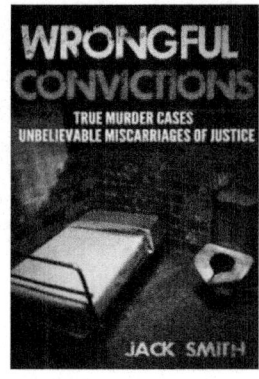

THE HAPPY FACE MURDERER

The Life of Serial Killer Keith Hunter Jesperson

Jack Smith

THE HORRIFIC CRIMES
GILLES DE RAIS
REVISITED

Life of a Serial Killer of the Middle Ages

Jack Smith

THE BEAST OF BIRKENSHAW

LIFE OF SERIAL KILLER PETER MANUEL

JACK SMITH

BODIES IN BARRELS
THE SNOWTOWN MURDERS

JACK SMITH

HIDDEN BRUTALITY

LIFE OF SERIAL KILLER CARL EUGENE WATTS

JACK SMITH

THE SPOKANE KILLER

The Life of Serial Killer Robert Lee Yates Jr.

Jack Smith

THE SCORECARD KILLER
LIFE OF SERIAL KILLER RANDY STEVEN KRAFT

JACK SMITH

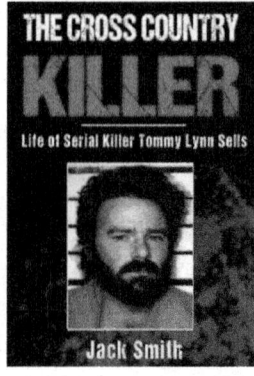

THE CROSS COUNTRY KILLER

Life of Serial Killer Tommy Lynn Sells

Jack Smith

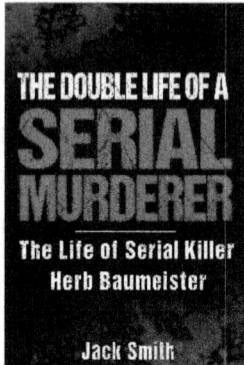

THE DOUBLE LIFE OF A SERIAL MURDERER

The Life of Serial Killer Herb Baumeister

Jack Smith

Printed in Dunstable, United Kingdom

76373225R00057